THE LIFE YOU'RE FIGHTING FOR

STRENGTH *and* STAMINA

to WIN *your* SPIRITUAL BATTLES

JAMES ROBISON

The Life You're Fighting For
Copyright © by LIFE Outreach International
All Rights Reserved

Published by LIFE Outreach International
P.O. Box 982000
Fort Worth, TX 76182–8000

Printed in the United States of America

ISBN 0-9653940-6-9

Unless otherwise noted, Scripture is taken from the Holy Bible, New
International Version ® NIV ®. Copyright ©1973, 1978, 1984 by
International Bible Society. Used by permission of Zondervan. All rights
reserved.

Scripture marked KJV is taken from the King James Version of the Bible.

Cover Design by INPROV

The Life You're Fighting For

James Robison

"Therefore repent and return, so that your sins may be wiped away, in order that times of refreshing may come from the presence of the Lord; and that He may send Jesus, the Christ appointed for you, whom heaven must receive until the period of restoration of all things about which God spoke by the mouth of His holy prophets from ancient time" Acts 3:19-21 (NASB).

Since God called me into ministry, nothing has thrilled me more than the message presented in the passage above. These are the days of restoration, the last great work of the Lord with His people before Christ returns to receive His Bride.

God has called us all to be an instrument in this exciting work. Our purpose is to help restore the Church to New Testament life, unite true believers and make disciples of Jesus Christ who will share His life with others. The vision is to see every believer led by love into oneness in Christ, then, in the power of His Spirit, reach the world with redemption through Jesus Christ.

This publication is designed to help you fight for and live a life of victory, to help you receive Christ's restoring ministry for your own life and to equip you to share the reality of abundant life available through Christ.

"Until we all attain to the unity of the faith, and of the knowledge of the Son of God, to a mature man, to the measure of the stature which belongs to the fullness of Christ" (Ephesians 4:13 NASB).

Chapter ONE

More Than A Conqueror

The Basis for Spiritual Warfare

"Spiritual warfare? What's that?"

Many Christians react in that puzzled manner to the subject of spiritual warfare. Some have never heard of it. Others have only the faintest understanding of what the term means. Most do not know they are involved in it, and very few realize to what extent.

For that reason, the first lesson most Christians need to learn about spiritual warfare is simply this: it's real. The battle is raging. And you are right in the middle of it.

"Where are the battles being fought?" you may ask. "Where is the spiritual warfare in my life?"

This may come as a shock to you, but it's in everything you do, think and feel. In spiritual warfare, there is no such thing as a "no man's land." Every area of the Christian life is involved in spiritual warfare: your worship and service in the church, your career, your personal relationship with the Lord, your health. In every facet of life, in every mental or physical activity in which you engage, spiritual warfare is raging.

If you are not aware that this war is on, it means just one thing: you are losing it. Before you can hope to turn the tide of the battle, you must acknowledge that the war is in progress and that you are a combatant — unknowing, ineffective and defeated though you may be.

The Reason for Spiritual Warfare

You may be saying, "All right, I acknowledge that I'm involved in a spiritual war, but why?" For two basic reasons: your identity and your purpose.

Consider first your identity. Who are you? Assuming that you are a born–again believer, the Bible says you are a child of God (John 1:12-13). As a child of God, you share His divine nature (2 Peter 1:4). Thus, in what you are, in your inmost personhood, you are different from the beings that populate the lost world. It is a characteristic of the nature of those lost beings to behave with

> *In spiritual warfare, there is no such thing as a "no man's land."*

suspicion and hostility toward anyone who differs from them, who does not seem to fit into their mold. To them, you are a "peculiar" person. Like chickens that peck the "different" member of the brood, they tend to attack you simply because of your nature — and theirs. Because of who you are, you also operate differently. The children of the world live according to sense–knowledge. Whatever their five senses can pick up from the world and whatever human logic they can apply to this data provide the guidance for their behavior. You are born again to live by the Word of God and by the guidance of the Holy Spirit. The world does not believe in the first and does not see the second (John 14:17). The more you function in accordance with your divine nature the more apparent the differences will be between you and the children of the world and the greater their animosity toward you may be.

You are involved in spiritual warfare, not just because of your identity as a child of God, but for another and more direct reason: because of your purpose.

What is your purpose in the world, as a child of God? Many Christians would say, "To live a Christian life," "To serve others," "To win others to Jesus" or just to go about doing good. None of those answers is wrong, but they don't fully express the gravity of your purpose either.

In 1 John 3:8, the Spirit reveals that Christ's purpose in coming into the world was "that He might destroy the works of the devil" (NKJV). Jesus tells us in John 20:21, "As the Father hath sent me, so I send you" (NASB). The word "as" means, among other things, "with the same purpose," so one purpose in your life is the same as Jesus' — to destroy the works of the devil.

The writer of Hebrews describes Christ's mission in this

manner: "[To] render powerless him who had the power of death, that is, the devil, and might free those who through fear of death were subject to slavery all their lives," (Hebrews 2:14-15 NASB). Then, in Chapter 3, verse 1, he identifies Christians as "partakers of the heavenly calling" (NASB). What is the heavenly calling? To destroy the works of the devil and deliver those whom he holds captive. You share that calling with Christ.

Many Christians are not aware of this purpose, their heavenly calling. But the enemy knows it, and he is continually doing everything in his considerable power to thwart that purpose. He has two major strategies:

1. To keep Christians blind to their purpose and unaware of the war waged against them.

2. To attack them at every opportunity and on every possible front with the intent to destroy them, or at least render them ineffective.

If Satan has been able to blind you to your purpose and keep you oblivious to the war he is waging against you, you may think you are escaping the conflict. If so, you're only deceiving yourself. Jesus said that because the enemy hated Him, he would hate you also (John 15:18). "In the world you have tribulation"

(John 16:33 NASB). These are certainties for the Christian. If you are not aware of them, it is only because you are not spiritually sensitive enough to realize how much of your heavenly goods — love, joy, peace, fellowship, and even provision — the enemy is plundering from you.

Our Credentials for Spiritual Warfare

Many of the great heroes of the faith, when first informed by God of His purpose for them, responded with fear and doubt. Take Moses, for example. After hearing God speak to him from the burning bush, his first words were: "Who am I, that I should go to Pharaoh, and that I should bring the sons of Israel out of Egypt?" (Exodus 3:11 NASB).

Perhaps after hearing about your purpose and the spiritual warfare in which you are entangled, you are asking: "Who am I, that I should take on the devil himself and go about destroying him and his works and setting free those he holds captive?"

If so, don't be ashamed. It's a good question. You need to know who you are in no uncertain terms before you go up against this clever and powerful enemy. The Lord knows well that our victory in spiritual warfare depends upon our knowing who we are and the grounds on which we justify our involvement in the conflict.

For that reason, God takes pains to clarify our identity, which is the primary basis for our warfare.

Who are you to be contesting Satan and delivering his captives? To answer that, God has told you that you are one with Christ.

"Christ . . . is our life," Paul wrote in Colossians 3:4. He overcomes the world, and in Him, we can be sure that we overcome it. We are in the world as Jesus was (1 John 4:17) — with the

same mission, to be sure, but also with the same power, authority and resources to

> *Many of the great heroes of the faith, when first informed by God of His purpose for them, responded with fear and doubt.*

carry out that mission. The power that raised Christ from the dead and set Him above all principalities and powers, in this world and the world to come, is the power that operates in you (Ephesians 1:19-21). This same power gave Jesus His victory, the crushing triumph that made Satan and his forces a laughingstock (Colossians 2:15). You are "strengthened with all power, according to His glorious might . . . " (Colossians 1:11 NASB).

You also have Christ's authority in waging spiritual warfare. Because of your identification with Him, you have been delegated "all authority in heaven and on earth" (Matthew 28:18, 20 NIV). In John 16:24, Jesus says, "Hitherto have ye asked nothing in my name: ask, and ye shall receive, that your joy may be full (KJV)." The word "ask" in the original language is stronger than the translation suggests. It could be rendered "demand" or even "command." It does not mean "demand" in an arrogant way, but in the sense that you would claim something you had a legal right to. For example, when you write a check on your own account at the bank, you are demanding a sum of your own money. But your check says, "Pay to the order of . . . "

The words "order" and "command" are synonymous. So, basically, you are commanding the repository of your money to release some of it for your use.

So what is Jesus saying, when He tells you to "ask" something in His name? He is saying you have a legal right to issue orders in His name. You have the authority to make demands on your heavenly resources. All that is His is yours, because you are a "joint heir" with Him (Romans 8:17). "Heir" is a legal term. It means these things are yours by right. What things? "All things that pertain to life and godliness," 2 Peter 1:3 says (NKJV). "All spiritual blessings in the heavenly places," according to Ephesians 1:3 (NKJV). You also have authority to issue commands to the heavenly hosts, the forces of the kingdom of God, as military commanders in the world order troops about in earthly combat.

The authority given you is the authority given Christ. This is your commission. In speaking of the Great Commission, many preachers start with Matthew 28:19: "Go ye therefore, and teach all nations, baptizing them in the name of the Father, and of the Son, and of the Holy Ghost" (KJV). But that actually is the mission, not the commission. The commission is found in verses 18 and 20, where Christ tells his followers of the power and authority given them to carry out the mission.

When a soldier graduates from West Point, the U.S. Military Academy, he doesn't just receive a mission — an assignment to defend the country against its enemies, foreign and domestic. He receives a commission. That means bars on the shoulders, credentials that authorize him to issue orders pertaining to the disposition of troops, weapons and resources — in the name of the commander-in-chief, the president.

God's army operates in precisely the same manner. As a commander in His army, you have a commission. And, just as President Roosevelt authorized General Eisenhower to issue orders in his name during World War II, the Lord Jesus, the captain of our salvation, is saying to you, in essence: "You have had those bars on your shoulders for a long time, but, until now, you haven't issued any orders in my name. Start issuing some commands, and let's get this war under way, so I can give you some victories to celebrate and your joy can be full."

Because so much emphasis has been placed on the mission and so little on the commission, many Christian warriors quail at the thought of spiritual warfare. The task looks so formidable and their own ability so limited that they try to avoid the conflict.

> *To make effective use of your weapons, you need to know the purpose of each piece and how it functions to fulfill that purpose in the heat of battle.*

If they would only listen to the Lord, and realize the total adequacy of their power, authority and resources through Him, they would be gung ho for taking on the enemy. They would relish the thought of battle, for each encounter means another victory, someone or something else liberated from the cruel captor, Satan.

The Weapons of Our Warfare

Many people have spoken and written about the Christian's armor Paul describes in Ephesians 6:11–18. Most treatments of the passage tend only to identify and explain the various pieces of armor, however, without detailing how and why they are effective in spiritual warfare. To make effective use of your weapons, you need to know the purpose of each piece and how it functions to fulfill that purpose in the heat of battle.

First, you should appreciate the fact that your armor is "of God" or "from God." The armor and weapons you carry into battle were manufactured by God, the most reputable supplier of armaments in the universe. In the United States Army, the weapons and equipment supplied each soldier are called "Government Issue," meaning they are the standard gear issued by the U.S. Government to its troops. From that fact came the term G.I., which became a nickname for the soldiers receiving the items. As a spiritual soldier, your gear is also G.I. — not government issue, but God Issue. It is the standard gear God provides for all His troops. It is the same equipment that He issued to Moses, Samson, Gideon, David, Jehoshaphat and all the others to whom He gave great victory. It is the same gear used by Jesus Christ the Lord, captain of our host!

Since our weapons have been fashioned and issued by God, they are spiritual weapons. That means they are supernatural, capable of withstanding and overcoming the "principalities . . . powers . . . rulers of the darkness . . . wicked authorities of the spiritual realm." The enemy's armor and weaponry are also supernatural. For us to be victorious, ours must be supernatural of an even higher order. And so they are.

The first word of instruction concerning our armor is to put it on. Without the protection issued by the Lord, we have no chance against the enemy's supernatural schemes and devices. Paul tells us to put on "the whole armor" — every piece of it. If you went charging into battle missing any piece of this armor, you would be vulnerable in some vital area to the devil's deadly darts. You must make use of everything God provides in your spiritual warfare. This is no brush fire battle or "police action." This is an all out war.

Now let's consider the various pieces of equipment God provides and the importance of each to our victory.

The Girdle

The first piece of armor Paul identifies is the girdle. This is the broad strip of plating or mail the warrior buckles around his waist. It covers his hips, stomach and abdomen. It also serves as the anchor for other pieces of the armor, which are linked to it, and as the hanger to which other gear and weapons are attached, such as the sword and the dagger.

For the spiritual warrior, Paul says, the girdle is truth. God's Word, of course, is the truth, but the Word of God is identified later as another part of the armament: namely, the Sword of the Spirit. In the case of the girdle, the word "truth" might best be understood as "reality." Now examine this girdle of reality in terms of spiritual warfare. One of the keys to victory in any battle is the ability to keep a firm grip on reality — to maintain an awareness of the true situation, to know what is going on. Many times, in Old Testament battles, God's enemies destroyed themselves. Because they lost touch with reality, they became disoriented and, in their confusion, fell on one another.

Because the Holy Spirit constantly gives you revelations of reality, you can avoid that horrible fate. By staying tuned in to God's version of reality, you can always know what is happening on the battlefield. This solid sense of reality holds your armor in place for you, keeps your weapons handy for use and fends off the confusion and panic that could be your undoing when you get into the thick of the fight.

The Breastplate

One of the most important pieces of armor worn by a spiritual warrior is the breastplate. The Roman soldier wore two metal plates that protected his upper torso in front and back and clamped together beneath his arms. This piece covered the heart, lungs, and other vital organs. No soldier of Paul's day would dream of going into battle without his breastplate in place.

The Christian's breastplate is his righteousness. Yes, that is the proper term: his righteousness. Righteousness is "from God" and is appropriated "by faith" (Romans 10:3,6 NIV). But, once so appropriated, it becomes the believer's own righteousness. In Christ, we have been made the righteousness of God (2 Corinthians 5:21).

Unless you have the breastplate of your righteousness, issued to you by God through faith, you are not likely to go into battle against the enemy at all. If you go, you will encounter almost instant defeat. Why? Because the weapons used by Satan, the accuser, most devastatingly against the Christian are of accusation and condemnation. When you plunge into battle, his first counterattack will probably be a fusillade of questions designed to undermine your confidence in your qualifications as a soldier of the Lord Jesus Christ.

The weapons used by Satan, the accuser, most devestatingly against the Christian are of accusation and condemnation.

"What makes you think you are good enough to make war against me? You're not perfect, are you? Don't you feel just a little phony, claiming to be righteous? Didn't I see you sin just a little while ago?"

You cannot withstand such an onslaught until you have firmly put on your breastplate of righteousness — that is, until you have chosen to believe what God has said about having made you a righteous being when He gave you a new birth and made you a new creation. You are His workmanship (Ephesians 2:10), and God's workshop doesn't turn out any unrighteous products.

By emphasizing so strongly the sin that crops up in the way Christians behave, our churches tend to say too little concerning the righteousness we have in Christ. The result is the Christian warrior's heightened sin-consciousness, when what he needs for effective spiritual warfare is to be more righteousness-conscious.

This error in emphasis keeps many Christians cowering behind the lines or, once having gone into battle, fleeing in panic after the first exchange of fire. If you don't know your own righteousness, you have no stomach for spiritual combat. You will always be hanging around the armory trying to beat out a breastplate that you hope will stand the test of battle. You'll never succeed. Only with righteousness that is of God will you have success. It cannot be worked up, even by the most skilled metal smith. The only way to receive it is to believe for it. It's G.I. — God Issue.

Once you have believed for your righteousness, you have a breastplate that will deflect anything the enemy hurls at you. Then, all you have to do is put it on and join the battle.

Footwear

It may seem strange that Paul mentions protection for the

feet in almost the same breath as armor for the more vital organs, the heart and lungs. He did so because he knew about military operations and what causes them to succeed or fail. He knew that an army will go nowhere — literally — unless the soldiers' feet are properly shod or dressed.

The Christian's footwear is "the gospel of peace." That is what carries you into battle — the Good News, the truth that sets men free, the glad tidings that can liberate the captives from the enemy. This is what saved you. This is what motivates you to want others to be saved. This is what keeps you moving forward against the enemy and his fortifications even when the terrain is rough.

The importance of this footwear points to another reason why the Christian army moves so slowly and inconsistently. The "gospel of peace" is good news; it is good tidings. Yet it is far too seldom presented as such. This good news most often comes across to the Christian warrior as gloomy news and bad tidings — toilsome works, guilt burdens and tongue–lashings. With that shoddy gear on his feet, the warrior is not likely to venture toward the battlefront. If he does, he probably will not get very far before he starts limping back to camp.

Putting the "gospel of peace" on your feet means receiving by faith the Good News of the New Testament, a covenant based on grace, mercy and eternal life, not works, condemnation and death.

" 'But this is the covenant which I will make with the house of Israel after those days', declares the Lord, 'I will put My law within them, and on their heart I will write it . . . They will not teach each man his neighbor . . . saying, "Know the Lord," for they will all know Me . . . ' " (Jeremiah 31:3334, NASB). "For I will be merciful to their unrighteousness, and their sins and their iniquities will I remember no more" (Hebrews 8:12, KJV).

That is the kind of footwear you can march in!

The thought of having your feet shod with the gospel of peace becomes all the more exciting when you realize that peace exists only after a battle has been fought and the enemy has been vanquished. Wearing the gospel of peace on our feet, then, means having one foot planted on the back of our defeated foe, and the other standing steadfast on the Word of God, through which we have been given the victory!

The Shield

Faith is the Christian warrior's shield. "Above all, taking the shield of faith," Paul said. That might better be read "over all" or "covering all." When the Roman soldier crouched behind his shield, it protected his entire body from head to foot. All of the soldiers with their shields in place, presented a veritable wall against an enemy's charge. Faith serves in like manner for the Christian in spiritual warfare.

Faith covers everything for the Christian in combat. Faith actually provides the armor and the weapons. And faith protects each item — the girdle of truth, the breastplate of righteousness, the footwear of the Gospel, the helmet of salvation, the sword of the Spirit. All depend on the shield of faith.

What is the shield of faith? Simply our belief in God, His Word, His Promises. By faith — believing what God has said — we know who we are, why we are engaged in this spiritual warfare, what we have to fight with and the ultimate triumphant outcome of the struggle.

The shield of faith quenches all the fiery darts of the wicked one, Paul says. What are those fiery darts? They are Satan's lies, deceptions and misrepresentations of reality. When we are using the shield of faith, we are believing God, and when we are believing God, we are rejecting the falsehoods flung at us by the enemy. All his fiery darts sputter and die when we use faith against them. They lose their sting. They cannot penetrate our armor or inflict any wounds upon us.

"Take the shield of faith," Paul exhorts. That is a command to action. Faith is an action word which connotes an exercise of the will, the deliberate act of choosing to believe God in the face of any conflicting statements or evidence, the enemy's "Fiery darts." By choosing to believe God, rather than the suggestions of the enemy, we take up the shield of faith.

You may think of yourself as a believer, but before you go into battle be sure to check your shield. Are you really believing what God has said — about who you are and what you have for waging this spiritual war? If not, beware. Satan's fiery darts of deceit will find the chinks in your armor!

The Helmet

To win in battle, a soldier must be sure not to lose his head! Literally, of course, but spiritually as well.

The helmet, that part of the armor that enables us to keep our heads, no matter how threatening and confusing the battle may become, is our salvation.

> *Putting on your helmet means knowing — through faith and the confirmation of the Holy Spirit — that you are saved.*

Putting on your helmet means knowing — again through faith and the confirmation of the Holy Spirit — that you are saved. That in turn means knowing and believing the simple truth as stated in the Psalms and numerous other passages: salvation is from the Lord. It is the gift of God, by grace through faith, and not of works. You did nothing to earn it. You can do nothing to keep it. All you did was receive it, and you did that through a faith that God gave you through Jesus Christ. God, and He alone, is able to keep it for you (2 Timothy 1:12).

If you don't put on your helmet of salvation, you will be disoriented regarding that basic aspect of your faith. You will be preoccupied with trying to do something to get saved and to keep yourself saved. Caught up in this self–centered activity, you won't be free to wage an effective fight to destroy the enemy's works and liberate others from his captivity. Moreover, you will be extremely vulnerable yourself. Without a helmet, your very head will be exposed to every missile the enemy aims at you.

The Sword

The sword of the Spirit is the last item on Paul's list of armaments, but that does not mean it is the least important. All the other pieces mentioned are strictly defensive in their functions. They are to protect you from the enemy's weapons. The sword is both offensive and defensive in function. With it, you can parry Satan's thrusts, as Jesus did during His wilderness temptation battle (Matthew 4:1–11). But the sword of the Spirit, the Word of God, is also our only offensive weapon. You are to wield your sword to put the enemy to flight and set his captives free.

To effectively use the sword, however, you must avoid the common misconceptions concerning it.

First, use of the sword does not consist merely of spouting Scripture. The devil himself can — and does — quote Scripture.

Speaking to some early-day Christians who were evidently quite adept at reciting Scripture and otherwise flaunting their "spirituality," Paul said: "But I will come to you shortly, if the Lord will, and will know, not the speech of them which are puffed up, but the power" (1 Corinthians 4:19 KJV). For the kingdom of God is not in word, but in power.

It is clear from many Scriptures that power is supplied by the Holy Spirit. After all, only when the sword of the spirit is wielded in union with Him, through complete dependence on Him, does the Word go forth with power. The apostles were instructed to wait in Jerusalem until the Holy Spirit had been given because only then would they have the power to perform their mission.

The key, then, to effective use of the sword is faith. The Word spoken in faith moves mountains (Mark 11:23). Jesus using the Word in faith calmed the wind and waves on the sea of Galilee after the disciples — reasoning without faith — had concluded that they would perish (Mark 4:35–41).

What happens when we have the Word without faith is best seen in the failure of the children of Israel to go into the Promised Land. They had the Word, but it was of no use to them because they did not combine it with faith, Hebrews 4:1 tells us. Because of their unbelief, their weapons were ineffective, and they failed to enter into God's rest — the wonderful peace that follows spiritual victory.

God's Word, based on His promises as revealed in the Scriptures and spoken in faith by the spiritual warrior, will activate the sword of the Spirit. And the enemy will not be able to withstand its power. Your capacity for spiritual warfare can be summed up by the words of Paul in 1 Corinthians 3:21, "All things are yours," (NKJV). All things. Your identity as a child of God and a sharer of the heavenly calling. Your authority. Your power. Your weaponry and your armor. You are fully equipped for the spiritual struggle in which you are involved. You CAN emerge victorious.

> *You are fully equipped for the spiritual struggle in which you are involved. You CAN emerge victorious.*

You are a Super Conqueror

In the light of this, Paul's words in Romans 8:37 take on a deeper significance for you, perhaps, than they ever have before. You are a super conqueror! Nothing the enemy throws at you can overcome you. No strength he can bring to bear is capable of resisting your power to destroy his works and deliver his captives.

There is one important point to remember: this is all true regardless of how you feel about it.

When the Lord appeared to Gideon, He introduced Gideon to himself [Gideon] as a "mighty man of valor." Gideon didn't feel mighty or brave. He argued with the Lord, saying, (my paraphrase): "My family is the poorest in all Israel, and I'm the poorest in the family. With puny resources like that, how could I be mighty? And I'm not very brave, either, Lord. Look where you've found me — hiding from the Midianites here behind the winepress!"

But the Lord said, "I am with you." And God worked with Gideon, building his confidence until Gideon believed what God said about him. Gideon was then able to prove himself a mighty man of valor and to deliver the Israelites from their Midianite oppressors. How did he do it? By leading a mere 300 men, armed only with lamps, sticks and pitchers, against the Midianite horde, numbering some 165,000. Because he finally believed the Lord was with him, he defeated that great host in one engagement (Judges 6–8)!

You are a mighty man of valor — or a mighty woman of valor — no matter how small and insignificant you may feel. "For we walk by faith, not by sight," Paul said (2 Corinthians

5:7 KJV). That means that we live according to what God says about things, not according to how we think or feel about them. That's faith, and faith "is the victory that has overcome the world" (1 John 5:4 NKJV).

Let God introduce you to yourself. He says you are super conqueror. Choose to believe Him. Step out to behave according to that belief, and you will begin to experience the incomparable excitement and gratification that come with victory in spiritual warfare.

If you feel inadequate, thank God even for that. He has to make us feel helpless in our human ability before we will look to Him. Hear His promise, "I am with you," and rely on His power to make us super conquerors.

Finally, remember that the real battlefield is one of prayer and petition. After exhorting us to put on the whole armor of God, Paul tells us how to put it on, keep it on, and use it most effectively in our warfare against the enemy and for one another:

"With all prayer and petition pray at all times in the Spirit, and with this in view, be on the alert with all perseverance and petition for all the saints" (Ephesians 6:18 NASB).

Beware of making prayer a struggle. Knowing the necessity of prayer, many Christians have fallen into Satan's subtle trap of relying on the length, volume and verbiage of formal prayers for their effectiveness in spiritual warfare. That kind of praying produces mental and physical fatigue, just as any other toilsome work does. Jesus' invitation to rest applies to prayer as much as to any other area of our spiritual experience, if not more. The prayer of faith releases the power of God. In prayer, as in anything else, faith is not works! To avoid the pitfall of the prayer struggle, remember that Jesus showed no strain in the prayers He prayed to perform some of His greatest miracles — feeding the five thousand, raising Lazarus from the dead, the countless healings recorded in the Gospels.

Paul's very words, when examined closely, suggest a prayer of faith and rest, rather than works and struggle. No one could pray "all the time" the laborious prayers that tax your mental and physical prowess. A part of praying "in the Spirit" means yielding to His power and trusting His wisdom.

The prayer of faith is constant communion with God, trust that God has welcomed you into His presence through Christ. This constant awareness of who you are, a child of God, gives you unwavering confidence that your Father knows your heart and considers every thought a prayer. Your mind and will are controlled by the Spirit, and whatever you ask in Jesus' name you shall receive. It is an uninterrupted conversation with your Abba, Father — the loving Heavenly Father who has assumed responsibility for your care (1 Peter 5:7).

The last phrases of Paul's instruction in Ephesians 6:18 contain an important reminder that none of us are alone in this spiritual combat. You are but one warrior in a vast army of believers, and you have responsibilities for your comrades in arms. " . . . With this in view, be on the alert with all perseverance and petition for all the saints," Paul said.

First, you can look on things from the heavenly viewpoint that you have through Christ. You are not "under the circumstances." You are "above," where your life is hidden with Christ in God (Colossians 3:3). Knowing you are secure in Him, you are free to turn your attention to the needs of others.

You are to be alert to those needs, like a faithful soldier in combat watching out for his buddies, warning them when they are in danger from the enemy, calling for supplies when they run low on ammunition or food, providing covering fire for them in the midst of battle, comforting them and giving first-aid when they are wounded. If the response to your petitions seems long in coming, you are to keep calling "with all perseverance" until supplies and reinforcements arrive. Angels of darkness may restrain the aid that is sent, as when the "prince of the kingdom of Persia" delayed the messenger who was responding to Daniel's prayer (Daniel 10:12–13). This is war. You must engage diligently in every phase of it!

The battlefield responsibility does not stop with the warrior fighting at your side. This responsibility extends to the company, the battalion, the regiment, the division, the entire army of God. You are to "petition for all the saints," Paul said.

Prayer and petition are the keys to success on the spiritual battlefield. Our standing with God and our confidence before the throne of grace are the keys to success in prayer and petition. For it is whatsoever we ask in prayer — believing not begging or struggling — that we receive. And the summation of all that we receive is victory.

This is war. You must engage diligently in every phase of it!

Chapter
TWO
Kingdoms in Conflict

The Keys to the Kingdom — Good News!

Burnout seems to be the single most common affliction in our culture today. People find themselves getting burned out in education, careers, entertainment, relationships, religion and life in general. Nothing seems to satisfy.

Even the various generations have burned out. The younger generation burned out when the young realized not only that youth didn't last but that youth wasn't everything worthwhile in life. The "Me" syndrome burned out when its devotees began to realize that a self–serving, self–indulging, self–centered, self–actualized life is a self–sickening life, because self can never live up to its billing. The "Now Generation" burned out when its followers discovered that Now has little meaning or gratification when it is not vitally attached to a Before and an After.

Everything men have thought or sought has failed to give meaning and fulfillment, that special "something" that makes it exciting and really worth living. Everything ultimately has led to burnout. Does that describe the life you are experiencing?

If so, don't despair. There is good news for you.

You see, burnout is not a new phenomenon. The world was burned out 2,000 years ago. People were already sick of man's answers to questions about life's purpose and meaning. Their religious activities and rituals with their tiresome works and futile, endless sacrifices, had long since grown stale and empty to them. They were like sheep without a shepherd, darting this way and that in search of peace and security.

At this moment of total burnout for mankind, God chose to send His Son, Jesus Christ, into the world. Christ's mission was to save man, not only from the burnout of eternal separation from love and life after death but also from the burnout of meaningless existence in this life.

When the world sees and understands what God has done, many will turn to His solution for a permanent cure for their burnout. Christians, many of whom suffer burnout from inadequate belief, will experience new and vibrant faith lives.

God's remedy for burnout is to transfer people from a dreary realm of death and darkness into the Kingdom of Light, from the dominion of the devil to the Kingdom of His beloved Son (Colossians 1:13). To those who know this basic truth and recognize their citizenship in God's Kingdom, there is never a dull moment! Life overflows with excitement, anticipation, fulfillment and gratification.

The Kingdom Comes

That, essentially, is what Christianity is: the invasion of earth's gloom by the Light of God's Kingdom, manifested first through Jesus Christ and then through all who believe in Him and make themselves available to Him.

The Gospel of Mark gives a clear, concise account of this invasion in its record of the life and ministry of Christ.

From the baptism of John to Jesus' ascension, Jesus' walk on the earth is essentially a revelation of the Kingdom of God and how it operates in the world. Christ's ministry provided salvation for all who put their trust in Him, of course, but that hardly detracts from the fact that His life, death, burial and resurrection depict the Kingdom of God.

Since salvation consists of being transferred from Satan's kingdom to God's Kingdom, Christians have citizenship in a different realm than people who are unsaved. Therefore, believers should not live in the same manner or from the same resources as they did before salvation.

They should know who they are, what their resources are and how they can function as citizens of the Kingdom of God. Mark offers a fast-moving documentary filled with this vital information.

It's Good News

The first thing Christians should understand concerning God's

Kingdom and their citizenship there is that the coming of the Kingdom to earth is good news. That statement may seem trite, but how often do we hear the Gospel presented as good news?

Just after His baptism and temptation by Satan, Jesus went into Galilee preaching the Gospel of the Kingdom of God (Mark 1:14). The word "gospel" means "good news." Jesus proclaimed it to be good news with every word He spoke, and He demonstrated it as good news in every action.

In verse 15, He announces that the Kingdom of God is "at hand." It's here, He is saying. It has come to you. Then He pleads for man to "repent" and "believe the Gospel." There it is again — the Gospel, the "good news."

"Repent" means to change the way you think and act, to turn from one approach to life and adopt another. Since Jesus' next word is an exhortation to "believe," it follows that His plea for repentance refers to the area of belief. He is saying, "Change your belief system; stop believing (or trusting) what you have been believing, and start believing (or trusting) the 'good news.'"

His words imply that what they had been believing was bad news. And certainly it was. In effect, they

> *Change your belief system; stop believing what you have been believing, and start believing the 'good news.'*

had been believing that the way to salvation was through keeping the law, every letter of it. Yet, because of their flawed human nature, they could not do so. Romans 8:3: "For what the law could not do, in that it was weak through the flesh, God sending His own Son in the likeness of sinful flesh, and for sin, condemned sin in the flesh" (KJV). All have sinned and fallen short of the glory of God, Romans 3:23 tells us. With men, salvation is impossible. This is what Jesus told the disciples after His encounter with the rich young ruler (Matthew 19:26). That is bad news. But He quickly adds that all things are possible with God, including salvation. That's the good news.

Citizens by Nature

Salvation is of the Lord (Psalm 3:8). It's a gift from God, presented to us through the Lord Jesus Christ (Romans 6:23b). "Christ" means "anointed one." He was anointed — that is appointed and empowered — to save us. As the Son of God, He had the nature of God. That's the only thing that could save us — a change of nature, of what we are in our innermost beings — from children of wrath (Ephesians 2:2) to children of God (1 John 3:1–2). We are saved by the life of Christ (Romans 5:10). God's own nature is imparted to us through Christ in salvation. We are "born again" (John 3:3). In giving us His life, He gives us the nature transplant that is necessary for our salvation. The baptism of Jesus (described in Mark 1:9–11) pictures this fantastic truth. His being placed under the water and raised again depicts the culmination of His own ministry in His death, burial and resurrection as atonement for our sins. But in a deeper sense, it represents the death, burial and resurrection of all believers with Christ. These are the truths revealed through Paul in Romans 6:3–11.

The "old man," the sin nature inherited from Adam, is put to death, so that we are no longer slaves to sin. Then we are raised with Him to a new life — His life — with the divine nature of God (2 Peter 1:4). Therefore, we can know that in our innermost beings, we are dead to sin and alive to God through Jesus Christ our Lord (Romans 6:11).

When Jesus came up from the baptismal waters, the Holy Spirit descended on Him like a dove, and God proclaimed from heaven, "This is My beloved Son, in whom I am well pleased" (Matthew 3:17 NKJV). What Christians need to know most is that, having gone through the death, burial and resurrection depicted in that baptism with Jesus, the same words apply to them. We are all His beloved sons and daughters in whom He is well pleased! The nature that was not pleasing to Him was the object of His wrath and was put to death with Christ when He became sin for us (2 Corinthians

5:21a). In the new nature He has given us, we are pleasing to Him, because we are one with Christ and have become the righteousness of God in Him (2 Corinthians 5:21b). What a liberating, energizing truth this is to any believer who will let the Spirit of God reveal it to him!

Are you beginning to see what good news the gospel? No more bondage to a sinful nature. No more fear about our destiny. No more oppressive burden of guilt. No more feeling rejected by a God whom we can hardly recognize as a loving Father.

Through Christ, God has done it all. It is finished. He saves those who come to God through Him (Hebrews 7:25). He offers this salvation to us as a gift. All we must do to receive salvation is repent — stop trusting in what we have been relying on (our own goodness, our own works) and start trusting in the finished work of Jesus Christ; stop believing the bad news and start believing the good news.

Immediately after announcing that the purpose of His ministry was to proclaim the good news of the Kingdom of God, Jesus begins to demonstrate how the kingdom is to operate in the world. Walking beside the Sea of Galilee, He sees Simon, Andrew, James and John, and He invites them to drop what they are doing and come with Him. He promises to change them. They were ordinary fishermen. "I will make you to become fishers of men," He said.

What does this tell us about the Kingdom of God and how it functions in the world? That it operates in and through people — people who, before undergoing the change brought by salvation, are just plain human beings. The Kingdom of God operates through all who answer Jesus' call to follow Him. That means looking to Him not only for forgiveness of sins and reconciliation with God, but also for the resources to live a full and triumphant life. Too much emphasis has been placed on our eternal life with God in heaven's "by and by." What should excite us most is that, in Christ, we have life now!

This knowledge is far more important than the excitement it might bring, however. There is a far more serious reason why Christians need to be aware of it. That reason is pinpointed in the test Jesus faced just after His baptism.

Mark 1:12–13 tells us that the Spirit drove Him, or impelled Him, to go into the wilderness. Alone there, except for "the wild beasts," He was tempted for forty days. Remember, this was immediately after He had publicly made Himself totally available to God in baptism and the Father had identified Him as His beloved Son.

Jesus' experience holds some significant lessons for the Christian in how the Kingdom of God operates.

Kingdoms Clashing

First, citizenship in God's Kingdom does not shelter the believer from temptation and adversity. In fact, citizenship assures that the believer will experience some tests that even the lost person does not face. Temptation came upon Jesus because He was the Son of God. When believers realize their identities in Christ and make themselves available to God, they often will encounter a wilderness experience. Some well-meaning Christians may share that the new believers' commitment would solve all their problems. That is true, but God often allows things to get worse before they get better. Christians need to understand such trials and the reasons for them. The basic reason is that they are children of God and, as such, they are targets for the fiery darts of the enemy.

" 'If ye were of the world, the world would love his own: but because ye are not of the world, but I have chosen you out of the world, therefore the world hateth you.

" 'Remember the word that I said unto you, "The servant is not greater than his lord." If they have persecuted me, they will also persecute you; if they have kept my saying, they will keep yours also' " (John 15:15-20 KJV).

The forces of the Kingdom of God have invaded the enemy's domain. We can expect him to resist with fury.

Another lesson taught by Jesus' temptation, however, is that the sons and daughters of God have what it takes to overcome temptation and repulse the most vicious attack the enemy can mount against them. In the midst of the assault, it may seem that we have only wild beasts with us as Jesus did during His temptation. But God always has His angels standing by to minister to us (Psalm 91:11). He never leaves or forsakes us (Hebrews 13:5).

That is why it is so important for Christians to know who they are and what they have as citizens of God's Kingdom. We have a supernatural enemy who will attack and try to destroy us. But if we use the power available to us, he cannot defeat us. In Luke 10:19, Jesus said, " 'Behold, I give unto you power to tread on serpents and scorpions, and over all the power of the enemy: and nothing shall by any means hurt you' " (KJV).

An attack from Satan — or any trying circumstance he might fling against us — should be recognized as just another opportunity for us to demonstrate our power over him. In the temptation experience, Jesus proved that the Kingdom of God triumphs over the kingdom of darkness when Christians know who they are and depend upon their heavenly resources.

In the remainder of this chapter, we will see Jesus provide a breathtaking glimpse of the Kingdom of God in action.

Everyone Is Eligible

First, as mentioned before, He reveals that the Kingdom will take ordinary people who come to Jesus in faith and will change and equip them for life in the Kingdom. An important point too often overlooked in evangelical circles is that Jesus promises to make the changes. "I

> *The Kingdom will take ordinary people who come to Jesus in faith and will change and equip them for life in the Kingdom.*

will make you to become fishers of men," He said (Mark 1:17 KJV). Many of the Church's evangelistic endeavors fail because they attempt to use programs or pulpit pressures to make people into fishers of men, or because they exhort believers to transform themselves into fishers of men. Only Christ can change a mere human being into a spiritual being capable of fishing for men. In its evangelism, the Church should be leading people to present themselves wholly to Christ and to allow Him to work the needed changes. Then fishing for men would be something Christians would do "naturally," not under duress or out of a sense of duty or guilt. The "catch" would be considerably larger than mere human ability could make, perhaps like that brought in by the disciples when they let Jesus tell them where to lower their nets (Luke 5:4–7).

"Now when he had left speaking, he said unto Simon, 'Launch out into the deep, and let down your nets for a draught.'

"And Simon answering said unto him, 'Master, we have toiled all the night, and have taken nothing: nevertheless at thy word I will let down the net.' And when they had this done, they enclosed a great multitude of fishes: and their net brake.

"And they beckoned unto their partners, which were in the other ship, that they should come and help them. And they came, and filled both the ships, so that they began to sink" (KJV). This is the power of God's Kingdom, as opposed to human ability.

Kingdom Power and Authority

In Mark 1:21–45, Jesus gives a marvelous demonstration of the authority and power of the Kingdom of God. These verses underscore the necessity of "obeying the Gospel" or turning from dependence on human resources and ability (which is sin) and living entirely through God's ability and resources. Jesus' actions are supernatural. They could be accomplished only through divine authority and power.

Even His teaching displayed supernatural characteristics. He didn't sound tentative and uncertain in the things He said, as the scribes did. He taught with authority (Mark 1:22). He knew what He was talking about because He had experienced it all in

His union with the Father.

When Jesus began revealing the Kingdom through His actions, it was with the same authority and confidence that was evident when He spoke. Appropriately, His first act was to overcome the enemy in a direct confrontation. In the very synagogue where He had been teaching, there was a man with an evil spirit. The demon screamed, "Let us alone; what have we to do with thee, thou Jesus of Nazareth? Art thou come to destroy us? I know thee who thou art, the Holy One of God" (Mark 1:24 KJV).

In His response, Jesus confirmed the testimony of the evil spirit concerning His identity by exercising the power of "the Holy One of God." He rebuked the demon and ordered it out of the man. The evil spirit had no choice but to obey, because Jesus possessed all authority in heaven (the invisible realm) and in earth (the visible realm) (Matthew 28:18).

In subsequent incidents, Jesus healed people who were sick with various diseases, beginning with Simon's mother–in–law and ending with a man stricken by leprosy, the most loathsome and incurable illness of that day. He also continued to cast out demons, liberating many of Satan's captives.

Both types of activity are routine operating procedure for those who are citizens of the Kingdom of God. In his sermon at the house of the centurion, Cornelius, Peter combines healing and deliverance under the umbrella of "healing" (Acts 10:38).

"God anointed Jesus of Nazareth with the Holy Ghost and with power: who went about doing good, and healing all that were oppressed of the devil; for God was with him" (KJV).

Whether it is manifested through diseases of the body or dominance over the personality, the oppression of Satan can be "healed" by the power and authority of the Son of God.

Disturbed Reactions

But what response did Jesus' dramatic revelation of the Kingdom of God receive? The people, including those in authority, were astonished by the firmness and confidence with which He spoke. They were frightened by this demonstration of supernatural power. It moved them to wonder among themselves: " 'What thing is this? What new doctrine is this? For with authority commandeth he even the unclean spirits, and they do obey him' " (Mark 1:27 KJV).

Too often, the religious people in the Church today react in the same manner when they see the power and authority of the Kingdom of God demonstrated. It shocks and disturbs them. Instead of responding with wonder, love and praise of the merciful God from whom the power flows, they respond with fear and anger. Often, these emotions, mixed with envy, move the modern–day "chief priest" and protectors of the religious status quo to turn on Kingdom operatives, just as they did with Jesus (Mark 15:10).

Simple logic should lead people to expect the Kingdom of God to be something a bit out of the ordinary, a bit unusual. Yet when men see it revealed, they can't understand what is happening. Because it is unusual and extraordinary — just as they should expect it to be — they can't accept it.

"Let favor be shewed to the wicked, yet will he not learn righteousness; in the land of uprightness will he deal unjustly, and will not behold the majesty of the Lord" (Isaiah 26:10 KJV).

Kingdom Magnetism

The result of Jesus' demonstration, however, was that the confused, hurting and burnt-out masses sought Him in such large numbers that He had to stop going into the cities. His presence created too many traffic jams. He stayed out in the countryside, where people came to Him from everywhere.

That is how the Kingdom of God operates, displaying love, authority and power that draw people to it. When they come, it lives up to its promises, ministers to their pain, frees them from bondage, and fulfills their needs and expectations.

When believers begin to let the Kingdom of God operate through themselves, they will see true evangelism in action. As long as Christians depend on human ability and wisdom and man–made programs, they will continue to get the pitiful results evident today. If the church were demonstrating the Kingdom of God, people wouldn't have time for programs. They would have their hands full ministering to the masses being drawn to Christ. They would be letting the world see the supernatural power and authority and the unlimited resources of the Kingdom of Heaven, and they would realize that this is what man kind hungers for. They would indeed be lifting up Christ. Then He would fulfill His promise: "And I, if I be lifted up from the earth, will draw all men unto me" (John 12:32 KJV).

Millions of diseased and oppressed people wait in agony to see the uplifted Jesus — to see the genuine love, compassion and acceptance

> *That is how the Kingdom of God operates, displaying love, authority and power that draw people to it.*

of Christ. If they could see Him, they would come as they did during His walk on earth — in such numbers that the cities could not accommodate them. And, like Christ, Kingdom people would have to withdraw to the countryside to receive them. If they could see His love, they would come, as did the leper in Mark 1:40, saying "You can make me clean" (NASB).

For Believers Only

Believers can lift up Christ today. They can demonstrate the same power and authority of the kingdom of God to heal the hurting and deliver the oppressed that Jesus had during His time on earth. "As my Father hath sent me, even so send I you," He said (John 20:21 KJV). In light of numerous other verses and the overall message of the New Testament, the "as" in that statements means with the same mission (to deliver the captives — Hebrews 2:15) and also with the same power and authority (Matthew 28:18,20) and the same resources (2 Peter 1:3).

But in order to reveal the Kingdom of God through our lives with power and strength, Christians must take the term "believers" literally. We must choose to believe God's Word concerning our identity as Kingdom citizens, our purpose and our resources in pursuing that purpose. We must choose to believe that Christ IS our life (Colossians 3:4). And we must choose to step out, to behave according to our belief.

> *We must choose to believe God's Word concerning our identity as Kingdom citizens.*

In other words: repent and believe the Gospel — the Good News! Exercising faith is simply an act of the will — a choice to trust God's Word and power.

So if you are willing to experience the Kingdom of God operating in and through your life, you may begin to do so — assuming you have previously received Christ as Savior and Lord — by praying a simple prayer of faith:

Heavenly Father, I believe that my old sin nature was crucified with Christ and that I have been raised in Him with a new nature — your divine nature. I believe that Christ IS my life now, and that you will demonstrate your power through me, as you did through Him during His earth walk, as I make myself available to you. I am now yielding my life totally to you. Thank you for the wonderful works you are going to do in me and through me, and for the many who are going to be healed and set free because of that work. In Jesus' name, Amen.

If you have prayed in this manner, your citizenship papers are now in order, and you have the credentials necessary to wage victorious spiritual warfare!

Chapter
THREE
Heaven's Firepower

The Scope of Our Power

Even believers who know their oneness with Christ often wince at the thought of engaging in spiritual warfare. They may have seen that they are children of God, joint heirs with Christ, kings and queens, yet when confronted by the enemy, their throats become dry and their knees begin to buckle. It is one thing to talk about spiritual warfare, but when the battle call is sounded and the fiery darts start whistling past our ears, the first thought may be: "Am I going to be able to stand the test? Do I really have what it takes to win?"

Our Father knows us quite well. Anticipating these moments of doubt and hesitation on the fringe of the battlefield, He has taken pains to inform us of the total adequacy of our power and authority.

Our Power Identified

From the Captain of our host, Jesus Christ, we receive a clear identification of our power. It is the power of nothing less than the Kingdom of God. When He set out on His earthly mission, Jesus proclaimed "the kingdom of God is at hand" (Mark 1:15 KJV). That's the spiritual version of saying, "The Marines have landed, and the situation is in hand."

With the first coming of Christ, the Kingdom of God, also identified as the Kingdom of Heaven, landed on earth. It was an invasion by God's kingdom into the enemy's realm, the Kingdom of Darkness.

Jesus lost no time in planting the flag and announcing, "The Kingdom of God has arrived — it is here!" He made the proclamation in Mark 1:15. Ironically, the forces of darkness heard it and understood the situation almost immediately. A demon speaks through a man at Capernaum, saying: " 'What have we to do with You, Jesus of Nazareth? Did you come to destroy us?' " (Mark 1:24 NKJV). But the disciples were slow to recognize the fact that Jesus had come to establish the Kingdom of Heaven, a spiritual kingdom, on earth. Many of His disciples even today still do not recognize it!

Blindness to the fact that our power base for spiritual warfare is the Kingdom of God results in many unnecessary victories for the enemy. To understand what it means to be a member of God's invasion force in the world, we can look at an illustration from human history — the Second World War. In World War II, the Axis Powers, the armies of Hitler's Germany and Mussolini's Italy, controlled much of Europe. Millions of Europeans who loved freedom were imprisoned in concentration camps. The unincarcerated masses were controlled by fear, manipulation, deception and intimidation.

The United States had committed itself to join with other free countries to defeat the cruel oppressors and liberate the captives. In pursuit of that commitment, a vast army was sent to invade Europe. With the best equipment and weaponry America could produce, this army went into battle having the total resources of the nation behind it — the manpower, the industrial might, the strength of the economy and the political and social structure, the morale of the population, the ideals and principles America had always stood for. Backed by that power and dedication, American and Allied forces crushed one of the most fearsome military machines the world had ever known.

> *Our culture's mindset hinders many Christians from understanding the power of God's kingdom.*

As invaders of Satan's spiritual kingdom, we can take comfort in the parallel between our own situation and that of the forces in World War II. We have the total support of the "nation" we represent — the Kingdom of God. All of its resources — its authority, its power, its weaponry, its provisions — have been committed to our use.

In the world, America, China and the former Soviet Union

were referred to as "super powers." But as citizens of the Kingdom of God, we represent not just a super power but a "supernatural power."

Psalm 22:27–28 describes the extent of the kingdom's power: "All the ends of the earth will remember and turn to the Lord, and all the families of the nations will worship before You. For the kingdom is the Lord's and He rules over the nations" (NASB).

The whole world will submit to His rule, says Psalm 66:4: "All the earth shall worship Thee" (KJV).

This is not a kingdom that will flourish for a time, then decline, as human powers have been known to do. "Thy kingdom is an everlasting kingdom, and thy dominion endureth throughout all generations" (Psalm 145:13 KJV).

Our culture's mindset hinders many Christians from understanding the power of God's kingdom. Western rational thought insists that anything real must be explainable in terms of the visible, the material or the "natural." Hence the popular axiom, "Seeing is believing."

Because they cannot see the Kingdom of God, many tend to think of it only as a metaphor, a figure of speech. They do not accept its reality intellectually, much less practically.

But when Jesus said, " 'My kingdom is not of this world' " (John 18:3 KJV), He didn't mean that it was any less real than the world. In His conversation with Nicodemus the Pharisee in John 3, He emphasizes that the kingdom can be seen but not with our natural eyes. "Unless one is born again he cannot see the kingdom of God" (John 3:3 NASB). The literal translation is "born from above." The Kingdom of God is quite real, but it is above the kingdoms of this world. It is supernatural — above nature — and it can be seen only by those who have received the supernatural birth and come into spiritual being with supernatural eyesight.

Jesus stresses this point again in Luke 17:20–21, where He answers the Pharisees who have questioned Him as to when the Kingdom of God will come. " 'The kingdom of God is not coming with signs to be observed; nor will they say, "Look, here it is!" or, 'There it is!' For behold, the kingdom of God is in your midst' " (NASB). The literal translation says "within you."

When Jesus uses illustrations from the visible world to describe the Kingdom of God, He is not using the real to depict the unreal. He is using visible reality to depict invisible reality. In His model prayer, when He prays, "Thy Kingdom come. Thy will be done in earth, as it is in heaven" (Matthew 6:10 KJV), He means that the invisible things of the heavenly realm should control and manifest themselves through the visible things of the earthly realm.

Paul exhorts us in 2 Corinthians 4:18 not to look at the visible things but at the invisible, because the "things which are seen are temporal; but the things which are not seen are eternal" (KJV). In other words, the Kingdom–of–God reality is more real than earthly reality because it is everlasting, while the visible reality will endure only for a time.

The reality of the Kingdom of God is revealed, not just by what Jesus and the disciples said but by what they did. Jesus was not content just to illuminate our minds concerning the Kingdom of God by preaching it. He also illustrated it before our eyes by practicing it.

Many churches, due to the Western mindset, have not thought of the Kingdom of God as a reality. The Kingdom of God is often regarded as something to preach, rather than practice. As a result, there has been a lot of talking about God's Kingdom but precious little walking in God's Kingdom. Jesus' ministry was a "show and tell" act. He not only told about the Kingdom, He demonstrated it.

And He meant for His disciples to follow that pattern. When He sent out the twelve and the seventy, He was giving us a "sneak preview" of how the Kingdom of God would operate after His ascension and after the Spirit of God was put in the heart of every believer. The Kingdom of God is not in words, Paul said, but in the demonstration of power and of the Spirit (1 Corinthians 2:4, 4:20).

Our Power Explained

Realizing that our power in spiritual warfare is the power and the might of the Kingdom of God, we should not be surprised at the extent of that power. The first disciples were surprised.

Jesus sent them out in Matthew 10:1, giving them "authority over unclean spirits, to cast them out, and to heal every kind of disease and every kind of sickness" (NASB). In verses 7 and 8, He makes it clear that this is to be a "show and tell" presentation of the Kingdom of God.

" 'And as you go, preach, saying, "The kingdom of heaven is at hand." Heal the sick, raise the dead, cleanse the lepers, cast out demons. Freely you received, freely give'" (Matthew 10:7–8 NASB). They were not just to talk about the kingdom. They were to demonstrate it.

Luke 10:17-19 reports what happened when they returned. The power they had experienced as they had obeyed Christ's instruction — the power of the Kingdom of God which Jesus had conferred on them — left them almost speechless.

" 'Lord, even the demons are subject to us in Your name,' " they exclaimed in awe.

Jesus, however, did not share their astonishment. He knew the extent of the power of the kingdom. He knew it had already crushed the enemy. " 'I was watching Satan fall from heaven like lightning' " (Luke 10:17–18 NASB), He said. He knew that when the enemy was flung from heaven, His power was broken. All power now belonged to the Son of Man and to whomever He would give it. Then He said to the disciples: "Behold, I have given you authority to tread upon serpents and scorpions, and over all the power of the enemy, and nothing will injure you" (Luke 10:19 NASB).

> *He knew that when the enemy was flung from heaven, his power was broken.*

That is the extent of the power of the Kingdom of God — the power given to all disciples of Jesus, all who believe in His name. This power is absolute. It is power to exercise total control over the enemy. This power assures that the enemy can do nothing to injure us, cripple us or put us out of action . . . provided, of course, that we know we have that power and that we step out in faith against the enemy to use it.

In Matthew 28:18–20, Jesus states the dual nature of kingdom power. It is not just power in the heavenly realm — the invisible or "spiritual" sphere. It is also power in the visible, material realm. " 'All authority has been given to Me in heaven and on earth', " He said, " 'and lo, I am with you always, even to the end of the age' " (NASB).

Most Christians go through their lives on earth in defeat because they don't understand that their power encompasses the physical as well as the spiritual. Thus, they will pray for the Lord to heal their bitterness but not their backaches. They will pray for relief from depression, as the victims of their emotions, but not for relief from oppression, as the victims of circumstances.

Ironically, the least spiritual among us sometimes spiritualize too much. When Jesus said, "Whoever says to this mountain, 'Be taken up and cast into the sea' . . . " the tendency of some is to quickly add to His words, "But, of course, not a literal mountain." What we must come to understand is that if we ever encounter a literal mountain that needs to be moved for the will of God to be done in our lives, it can be moved. All power in heaven and in earth means just that — all power. Believers do not have to live under their circumstances.

Jesus' words of explanation to the disciples in Matthew 16:19 give us some insight into how kingdom power works in the heavenly and earthly realm simultaneously. He says, "I will give you the keys of the kingdom of heaven; and whatever you bind on earth shall have been bound in heaven, and what you loose on earth shall have been loosed in heaven" (NASB).

When we speak a command in the visible realm through our natural bodies, it is carried out in the invisible realm by the supernatural power of the kingdom. And the results may well be manifested in the visible realm as well. What a marvelous revelation of our power for spiritual warfare!

The Lord presents a vivid action picture of the supernatural power of the Kingdom of God operating in the visible world through a man living in a flesh and blood, natural body. It's found in 2 Kings 6:8–23.

The king of Aram (identified as Syria in the King James Version) is attacking Israel, but his plans keep going awry. He has a terrible security leak. Every time he orders his troops to attack the Israelites, the prophet Elisha, tuning in through the Holy Spirit, picks up the message. The Israelites are warned and escape the trap. Growing weary of this, the king dispatches a great army, complete with horses and chariots, to Dothan with orders to take the prophet.

Early one morning, Elisha's young attendant gets out of bed, walks outside to stretch himself and sees to his horror a massive Aramean army encircling the city. He runs back inside, crying to Elisha, "Alas, my master! What shall we do?"

Elisha calmly reassures him: "Do not fear, for those who are with us are more than those who are with them."

You can imagine the young man's reaction. He looks again at the thousands of Aramean troops. He looks at Elisha. "That's one," he says to himself. Then he points to himself and says, "That makes two." Then he asks himself, "How can two be more than that multitude?"

Apparently noticing the young man's bewilderment, Elisha turns to the Lord, no doubt with a knowing smile on his face, and says: "O Lord, I pray, open his eyes that he may see."

The remainder of verse 17 gives the brief but electrifying account of what happened: "And the Lord opened the servant's eyes and he saw; and behold, the mountain was full of horses and chariots of fire all around Elisha."

That's what the Lord Jesus, the captain of our host, is asking God to do for us: open our eyes that we may see. In assuring us that He has given us all power over the enemy, He is saying: "Open their eyes that they may see."

When the enemy comes against us with frustrations, irritations and all manner of oppression, God is saying, "Open their eyes that they may see." When circumstances seem overwhelming and relief impossible, God is saying, "Open their eyes that they may see." When Satan assaults us with mental confusion or physical illness, God is saying, "Open their eyes that they may see."

If we open our eyes to see what the Lord is telling us about who we are and the power we have to do battle, no matter how great the demonic host sent to encircle us, we will always know that there is nothing to fear — that "those who are with us are more than those who are with them."

Let God open your eyes to who you are and the host that fights alongside you, and you will see the same electrifying sight that Elisha's young servant beheld that morning at Dothan. Encamped on your

> *Let God open your eyes to who you are and the host that fights alongside you.*

lawn or around your office or in your school, you will see a contingent of that same heavenly army, armed to the teeth with flaming swords and chariots of fire — the special operation troops of the King's honor guard, assigned to protect you, to march forth at your command to disarm or destroy any attacking force!

This episode in Elisha's life shows perhaps more clearly than any passage of Scripture the dual nature of our reality as citizens of the Kingdom of God. The kingdom is, indeed, at hand. It's right here with us — all around us. If we issue a command to that host in Jesus' name, a contingent marches forth to carry out our orders in the invisible realm — to bind, to loose, to lay siege on an enemy stronghold, to rip the scales from unseeing eyes and give sight to the blind, to bandage the injuries of the wounded, to liberate the captives.

Spiritual warfare becomes real for us when we get this picture. Not only real, but exciting! If there are always more of us than of the enemy — more in number, more in strength — then we can only be victorious if we join the battle.

Our Power Demonstrated

Our kingdom power for waging spiritual warfare that affects the visible as well as the invisible realm is clearly demonstrated in 2 Chronicles 20. A combined force of Moabites, Ammonites and Meunites has seized Jerusalem, where Jehoshaphat reigns as king of Judah. In terror, the king calls the people together to seek the Lord. He makes no effort to disguise his fear or instill false hope in the people with a show of bravado. He humbles himself before the Lord and his trembling subjects and prays:

"O Lord, the God of our fathers, are You not God in the heavens? And are You not ruler over all the kingdoms of the nations? Power and might are in Your hand so that no one can stand against You" (Verse 6 NASB).

Jehoshaphat knows the power of the Kingdom of God. He knows that it holds sway over kingdoms and nations in the visible realm as well as over invisible principalities and that no force is able to withstand it. But he is like many of us in that he is not quite sure that the power is his. He is not certain that God will release power on his behalf.

Perhaps his uncertainty stemmed from the fact that he had not conducted himself with flawless honor. He had ignored the Word of God, spoken through the prophet Micaiah (2 Chronicles 18) and gone into battle with Ahab, king of Israel, with whom he had allied himself by marriage. God had intervened to deliver him from what appeared to be certain death (Verse 31). When he returned safely to Jerusalem, Jehu the prophet came to him with a reprimand, "Should you help the wicked and love those who hate the Lord and so bring wrath on yourself from the Lord? But there is some good in you, for you have removed the Asheroth from the land and you have set your heart to seek God" (19:2–3 NASB). Like most of us, Jehoshaphat had done some good, but his performance was far from perfect.

Jehoshaphat also may have been guilty of depending on human power for defense against the enemies of the land. His first act after assuming the throne apparently was to turn the country into an armed camp, fortifying all the cities and establishing garrisons throughout Judah and Ephraim (17:2). As his kingdom grew richer, he devoted a large portion of the national budget to defense. The military buildup is documented in 2 Chronicles 17:13–19. Jehoshaphat may have misinterpreted the peace his land enjoyed as proof of the success of his man–made defense efforts. But the Lord showed us the true explanation of why the nations around Judah "did not make war against Jehoshaphat." It was because "the dread of the Lord was on all the kingdoms of the lands" (17:10 NASB) in the region. It was God's protection that held them at bay, not Jehoshaphat's troops and fortresses.

When the crisis came, however, the Lord did not answer Jehoshaphat on the basis of his performance. He did not review his past record to determine whether or not he was worth saving. It was enough for a loving and merciful God that the king had set his heart to seek God.

> *The king had set his heart to seek God.*

"For whoever will call on the name of the Lord will be saved" (Romans 10:13 NASB).

What a marvelous demonstration of the grace of God! Please remember this when you are confronted by the enemy and forced either to take your stand or succumb to his plundering. You may have erred many times in the past — even in the past five minutes! But you are still one of God's warriors, and

He will not desert you in the face of the enemy and leave you to be overrun by the forces of darkness.

Jehoshaphat threw himself upon that grace when he called on the Lord, saying: "O our God, wilt thou not judge them? For we have no might against this great company that cometh against us; neither know we what to do: but our eyes are upon thee" (2 Chronicles 20:12 KJV). By his actions, he acknowledged that all his military preparations were of no value in this crisis. Either God would save, or all was lost.

The crowd then waited in silence to learn what God's answer would be. You may be able to identify with them, as they stand there with the enemy closing in, wondering if God is going to come through . . . if the power of His kingdom will be available to them in this "do or die" moment.

Finally from the midst of the assembly, the Spirit of the Lord chose a spokesman — "Jahaziel, the son of Zechariah, the son of Benaiah, the son of Jeiel, the son of Mattaniah, a Levite of the sons of Asaph" (Verse 14 KJV). Jahaziel may have been so elaborately identified because his name was not exactly a household word in Jerusalem. From the mouth of this commoner, a member of the rank and file, God brought His message for the king: " 'Listen, all Judah and the inhabitants of Jerusalem and King Jehoshaphat: thus says the Lord to you,

"Do not fear or be dismayed because of this great multitude, for the battle is not yours but God's" ' " (Verse 15 NASB).

Whew! God is with us. Not only is He with us, but He is going to take responsibility for the battle.

Jahaziel goes on to outline the battle plan. This may be the strangest combat briefing in the history of warfare. Through His spokesman, the commanding General informs His troops that they are to go out and face the enemy but that they are not to fight.

"Tomorrow go down against them. Behold, they will come up by the ascent of Ziz, and you will find them at the end of the valley in front of the wilderness of Jeruel.

"You need not fight in this battle; station yourselves, stand and see the salvation of the Lord on your behalf, O Judah and Jerusalem? Do not fear or be dismayed; tomorrow go out to face them, for the Lord is with you" (Verse 16–17 NASB).

As strange as those marching orders sounded, Jehoshaphat and his people obeyed. They left their man–made fortifications and went out to face an enemy of apparently overwhelming strength. They went with no intention of attacking or even defending themselves. Instead, they divided the army into choirs, passed out the hymnals and began singing victory choruses and praising the Lord for crushing the enemy — before the battle had begun (Verse 20–22).

That was the signal for the Lord to attack. He set ambushes against the invading hosts, and they were routed, destroying one another. When the people of Judah looked up from praising God, what had once been a fearsome horde was a field strewn with corpses. And the spoils were more than God's people could carry back to Jerusalem!

In this incident, God reveals many lessons concerning spiritual warfare. Some of the most important lessons are summarized in Psalm 37:5–7. The passage contains four imperatives — commit, trust, rest and wait.

The people had to commit themselves to the Lord and show up at the battle. Humanly speaking, this involved great risk. They could have been humiliated and destroyed by that overwhelming force, if they had been depending on their natural ability to stand against it. That is how it will be with you in spiritual warfare. From the standpoint of your human ability, you don't have a chance. But you do have a prayer. If you use that prayer to commit yourself and the situation to the Lord and then go out against the enemy, God promises that He will do the fighting with the power of His kingdom. Your part, like that of the people of Judah, is to trust Him, rest and wait, celebrating the victory with song and praise. The Lord will take care of the enemy! What could be more exciting!

Jehoshaphat's experience also conveys a broader lesson that any believer waging spiritual warfare would be wise to keep in mind. It provides a glimpse of the heavenly and earthly realities coexisting and interacting with each other. God's warfare in the invisible sphere most certainly impacted the visible sphere. If you doubt that, ask the Moabites, Ammonites and Meunites. Or maybe it would be better to ask King Jehoshaphat and his people, who were delivered by the measures God took in the invisible realm — and were the only ones left to tell about it.

With the power and authority we have to bind and loose in the invisible realm, we can command demons to loose those

God's warfare in the invisible sphere most certainly impacted the visible sphere.

whom they are possessing or oppressing, and they obey. When they depart, we will see in the visible realm observable evidence that the person has been loosed. If we order Satan or any of his demons bound from individuals and situations, we will observe visible evidence that they have been restrained from their harassment or assault. This was demonstrated in Jesus' ministry, as in the case of the Gerasene demonic legion (Mark 5:15). Remember, when Jesus was on earth, He gave us a preview of what our lives and ministries are to be like.

Whatever we command in the visible world will be done in the invisible realm. The evidence of this being accomplished

— though perhaps not always — will be observable in the visible world. A word of warning would be appropriate at this point: our failure to see visible evidence should not cause us to doubt that the command is being carried out. We do not live by or base our conclusions on evidence gathered only by our senses. We walk by faith, not by sight (2 Corinthians 5:7).

Power Over Physical Affliction

A thorough discussion of physical healing will have to be reserved for a work of greater length, but the subject demands some attention in any serious study of spiritual warfare. Satan can and does come against us with disease and physical discomfort in an effort to discourage and defeat us. Job, of course, is the classic example of this type of satanic assault.

One important aspect of our redemption in Christ Jesus is the removal of the curse of the law and its effects on our bodies. Thus, Isaiah 53:3–4 informs us that Jesus bore our sicknesses and diseases and that by His scourging we have been healed.

In practical everyday living, this means that we do not have to tolerate the physical oppression Satan tries to place on us. We can, in the power of the Kingdom of God and in the name of Jesus, rebuke the devil, command the sickness to leave and the symptoms to disappear and receive the healing of the Great Physician in our bodies.

We do this in the same way we wage spiritual warfare on every other front. First, we remember who we are in Christ — we are children of God and joint heirs with Jesus, operating in this world with the same power, authority and resources He demonstrated while on earth. Knowing who we are, we realize that we are among those whose diseases and pains Jesus has already borne. We know that God would not put back upon us something the Lord Jesus has taken away with His sacrifice on the cross. Yet, we refuse to receive it.

Another, most important reason we know that we need not tolerate disease, not only in ourselves but in others is: it is God's will for the sick and afflicted to be healed.

This we know without doubt because Jesus and the Father are one. Jesus' life reflects God's life. " 'Whatever the Father does, these things the Son also does in like manner' " (John 5:19 NASB). Therefore, we can know God wants to heal, because Jesus' ministry was filled with healing. He healed "every kind of disease and every kind of sickness among the people" (Matthew 4:23 NASB).

Not only did Jesus heal, but He also empowered and commanded His disciples to do so. "Jesus summoned His twelve disciples and gave them authority over unclean spirits, to cast them out, and to heal every kind of diseases and every kind of sickness" (Matthew 10:1 NASB).

This sending out of the twelve was a demonstration of how God's people were to function in the Kingdom of God after Jesus' resurrection and ascension. His last words to the disciples included the statement that certain signs would accompany those who believe in His name. Among those signs was that "they will lay hands on the sick, and they will recover" (Mark 16:18 NASB). And, of course, in John 14:12 He said " ' . . . the works that I do, he will do also' " (NASB).

In the book of Acts, we find the apostles fulfilling that prophesy. Acts 5:15 records that the sick were laid along the streets so that Peter's shadow might fall on them and they would be healed. Handkerchiefs and aprons of the sick were sent to Paul, according to Acts 19:12, and their diseases and evil spirits left them.

Through the Apostle James, the Holy Spirit speaks clearly concerning not only our ability but our responsibility in the matter of healing. James 5:14–15: "Is anyone among you sick? Then he must call for the elders of the church and they are to pray over him, anointing him with oil in the name of the Lord; and the prayer offered in faith will restore the one who is sick, and the Lord will raise him up, and if he has committed sins, they will be forgiven him" (NASB).

If we fail to take a stand and exercise our powers over the physical body, we leave a most important front undefended against the merciless assaults of the enemy. God never intended us to accept such vulnerability.

Casey Treat, pastor of an 8,000-member, multicultural church in Seattle, Washington, found himself in a life–threatening situation a few years ago. Despite the many years he had spent serving the Lord and preaching the Gospel, his past came back unexpectedly to nearly destroy him.

During a routine exam, his doctor noticed that Casey's enzyme levels were "a little off." More tests revealed that he had Hepatitis C, an often incurable virus that destroys the liver. Medical reports reveal that the Hepatitis C virus has become an epidemic as people, now in their forties, reap what was sown in their youth.

After a thorough interview, the doctors concluded that Casey had contracted the virus in his youth from sharing needles while abusing drugs. The doctors explained that Hepatitis C lives in a person's cells indefinitely and slowly multiplies until it destroys the liver. Casey's medical team recommended a treatment program that gave him only a 4 percent chance of clearing the virus.

Casey reflected on how years ago, he had to make another life or death decision. He was on a path to destruction because of drugs.

"When I was nineteen," Casey said, "the judge said he would let me stay out of prison if I would stay in the rehab center. I told the judge that I would be there a while!"

Casey got more than he expected from rehab. The director told him, "I've got something more for you than drug rehab." Young Casey was born again and called to ministry, and the rehab director became his spiritual dad.

Casey earned a theology degree, started a radio broadcast and television program, founded Dominion College and led an international leadership conference. Then his life and ministry drastically changed as he and his family attacked the illness in every way. "God gives us many tools to face our problems," he said, "and I decided to use them all."

He believes in prayer and faith for healing. He had seen God work many miracles as he preached and prayed over people's physical needs. However, when he told his congregation about his illness, one of the doctors in his church showed him Proverbs 18:9 in the Amplified Bible. It says, **"Use every endeavor to heal yourself** lest you be brother to him who commits suicide."

"When I read that, God spoke to me," Treat said. "He told me not to put Him in a box, thinking that I will be healed by brother what's–his–name putting his hand on me, or sending off for the prayer cloth."

Casey felt if he used every endeavor, God would heal him in every way. He committed to a nutrition program, with supplements and vitamins, as well as the prescribed medical treatment. He also vowed to fight spiritually.

"Chemotherapy can put you in such darkness," he admitted. "But I stayed up as much as I could. I kept my prayer life strong and I stayed in God's Word."

When the doctors asked how he maintained such a positive mental state, he responded, "I keep my mind on Jesus, on His promise and on hope." The medical team didn't know how to process his answer, but they acknowledged they saw a difference in his experience with the treatment.

Pastor Treat believes that people are often waiting for God to do something in their lives in certain way; if

> *It is important to remember that our bodies are God's temple, and we should give due attention to caring for it.*

it doesn't happen in that way, they think God is not there. "God has many ways to get to us, and he uses many tools," he said.

The apostle Paul talked about being beaten, stoned, shipwrecked, forgotten and hungry, but he defined his greatness by his trials and his struggles. He concluded, "Most gladly, therefore, I will rather boast about my weaknesses, that the power of Christ may dwell in me"

(2 Corinthians 12:9b).

Casey advises people to let God bring them to the end of themselves — whether it is disease, a family problem or a financial problem. "When you come to the end of your strength, ask God, 'What can you do with me?' " Christians get stronger and better by journeying through battles with total dependence on His strength and His plan. The comfort and strength we gain is then passed onto others in prayers and encouragement.

After eleven months, Pastor Treat's family, friends and church members rejoiced as he was healed of Hepatitis C. "Now I've got pastors around America and around the world that I call every week," he said. "They're on chemotherapy for something or they're fighting other issues. Sometimes they just need to hear me say, 'Hey, I'm with you, man.' The prayer keeps them going." It is important to remember that our bodies are God's temple, and we should give due attention to caring for it. We often ask God to heal conditions related to poor health while we continuously neglect His dwelling place.

I am certain there will be occasions when we learn through sickness and suffering as Job and the apostle Paul did.

Remember, we follow a God of miracles, and a miracle of grace and power is needed and available when the requested healing miracle is delayed or unseen.

Chapter FOUR
Winning the War Within

Destroying Strongholds

To Christians, no aspect of spiritual warfare is more important than the destruction of strongholds in their personal lives and the lives of other believers. Many authors use 2 Corinthians 10:1–5 as a basic text when writing on strongholds. Some of these studies have been enlightening, but most contain one or more serious errors or shortcomings. This treatment probably is not the last word since the Holy Spirit seems to be continually shedding new light on the subject. But it should help equip you to wage successful warfare against spiritual strongholds.

What is a Spiritual Stronghold?

In 2 Corinthians 10:1–2, the Apostle Paul warns the believers to which he's writing that he will turn his spiritual guns on them if forced.

"But I beseech you," he says in verse 2, "that I may not be bold when I am present with that confidence, wherewith I think to be bold against some, which think of us as if we walked according to the flesh (KJV). He goes on to explain in verses 3 through 5.

"For though we walk in the flesh, we do not war after the flesh (For the weapons of our warfare are not carnal, but mighty through God to the pulling down of strongholds;) Casting down imaginations, and every high thing that exalteth itself against the knowledge of God, and bringing into captivity every thought to the obedience of Christ" (KJV).

Key words in the passage clearly indicate that Paul is talking about something in the minds of his readers when he speaks of "strongholds." In verse 2, he refers to the manner in which some think. Thinking is, of course, a function of the mind. Then, in verse 5, he speaks of imaginations, the knowledge of God and "every thought" — all of which point to the mind. But what, specifically, is Paul identifying with the use of the term "strongholds"?

> *To Christians, no aspect of spiritual warfare is more important than the destruction of strongholds in their personal lives.*

To answer that, we must first grasp the biblical model of the triune man. Man consists of spirit, soul and body. The spirit is our nature, what we are. The soul is our personality, how we think, feel and behave. And the body, of course, is the physical housing of the spirit and soul.

Since Paul clearly refers to thoughts in speaking of strongholds, he is talking about something in the soul, then, and not anything in the spirit.

This is reinforced by Romans 7:20–23, where Paul says that

when he does not behave as he knows in his heart to behave, it is "no more I that do it" (KJV). The sinful action does not originate from Paul's nature or spirit, from what he is. The regenerate spirit of the Christian, which shares the nature of God (2 Peter 1:4), does not produce sin. 1 John 3:9 says, "Whosoever is born of God doth not commit sin" (KJV), and 1 Peter 1:23 explains why: because he is "born again, not of corruptible seed, but of incorruptible, by the word of God, which liveth and abideth for ever" (KJV).

However, this is not a doctrine of "sinless perfection." The Bible makes it quite plain in numerous passages that the Christian's life can display sinful conduct. Although this sinful behavior does not originate from the spirit, where the believer's true identity lies, it must be recognized and dealt with. And that entails, first of all, understanding what the sinful behavior is and where it originates.

Paul says in Romans 7:23, that sinful behavior originates from "sin which is in my members" (KJV). Since it does not originate from the spirit, the "members" to which Paul refers must be the soul and body. Paul says there is a "law of sin" that lives within those

> *The regenerate spirit of the Christian, which shares the nature of God, does not produce sin.*

members, producing the sinful behavior. The word "law," as used here, connotes not a written code but a principle, as in the "law of gravity." From this it can be deduced that Paul is identifying a force or principle that operates in the soul (mind, will and emotions) and in the body, always driving the individual to behave contrary to the promptings of the Spirit, which is one with Christ and with God.

Combining all these insights, the "strongholds" Paul speaks of in 2 Corinthians 10 can be seen as the specific thought patterns, emotional patterns and resulting physical responses that the sin principle produces in the life of an individual.

The passage seems to contain nothing to justify some biblical teaching that strongholds are demons. Paul certainly knew the word "demons." He surely meant to communicate his Spirit–inspired insight clearly on such an important subject. Had he been referring to demons, Paul would have said "demons." Satan and his demonic cohorts can and do work from the outside to reinforce strongholds and create diversions to keep believers from using spiritual weapons to destroy them. (We can also triumph over these external activities and harassments through the power we have been given as spiritual commanders.) But to believe that we are warring against demonic beings within our souls when this is not the case would be to fight ignorantly and to risk tragic defeat.

For example, if we ascribe every spiritual problem to a demon, when we have exercised our power to cast out the demon associated with a given problem, the problem should go away. If the problem remains — and often it does — our faith may be undermined unless we understand that it may be the result of a structure (stronghold), not demonic activity.

Of course, this is not to say that Satan and his demons have had nothing to do with strongholds. The sin principle and the thought and behavior patterns that express it, were planted in the believer before salvation with the cooperation of the self-centered nature inherited from Adam. That nature, the nature of the devil himself, dwells in the spirit of every human being at the time of physical birth. Satan exercises control over the programming of our souls as we grow up and develop our personalities through his access to our spirit.

In Ephesians 2:2, Paul makes this point clear. Before Christ saved us, he says, we "walked according to the course of this world, according to the prince of the power of the air (Satan), the spirit that now worketh in the children of disobedience" (KJV). In other words, during our lives as unsaved persons, Satan, working through the self-centered spirit that was then our nature and the source of our identities (our "father, the devil" — John 8:44 KJV), programmed and conditioned our souls and bodies according to the devil's perspective on life and his strategy for fulfilling his evil purposes.

"Strongholds" are the particular strategies that were established in our souls during the period when we were "slaves to sin" (Romans 6:17 NASB). Because of the revolutionary change that occurs in the spirit at salvation, many of the satanic patterns or strategies are blasted away. But many still stand. These satanic patterns or strategies that remain in the soul of the believer are the strongholds at which Paul takes aim in 2 Corinthians 10.

Examples of Strongholds

Paul lists some examples of strongholds in Ephesians 4:22–32, where he is urging believers to "put off" the things that pertained to the "old man" (KJV), or the "spirit of disobedience" which we had before salvation. Now that the self–centered nature has been crucified with Christ, he is saying we should lay aside those things that were programmed into the soul when we had the old nature. The things he mentions include lying, stealing, corrupt communication, bitterness, wrath, anger, clamor, evil speaking and malice.

The self-centered nature wants everything to go its way. Anything that does not do so produces frustration. The self–nature's reaction to frustration is some form of hostility, either projected out or held in. Everything on the above list is an expression of either outward or inward hostility.

In general terms then, a stronghold can be defined as any thought, response or behavior pattern that either lashes out or seethes within when things don't go our way. Anger held in often produces physical strongholds, such as drug addictions and alcoholism. But these and other physical conditions are simply visible symptoms of the real stronghold, which is dealing with frustration by attempting to escape it.

Characteristics of Strongholds

Christians would do well to remember that strongholds are works of Satan. They are serious business. Jesus said the devil has come only to steal, kill and destroy (John 10:10). His strongholds are all designed to bring about destruction in our lives. They can steal our joy and peace, kill our relationships with others and destroy our opportunities to enjoy the abundant life God has given us through Christ. Ultimately, they can destroy us and the people around us. When you feel a tendency to joke or even boast about a stronghold — "my temper," "my greed,"

> *Behavior that seems to be handling you, rather than you handling it are strongholds.*

"my lust," "my disorderliness," for example — you are playing into Satan's hands. The last thing he wants is for you to see the sinister nature of these works and turn to God to have them destroyed.

Because these are Satan's works, strongholds display distinct characteristics. To name a few:

Strongholds are stubborn. They seem impossible to break down. Attacked with humanistic programs and approaches, they may appear to weaken or vanish temporarily only to re–emerge, sometimes stronger than before. They do not yield to attacks based on religious activities. After years of trying, people often give up all efforts to get rid of them and simply "learn to live with them."

Strongholds are irrational. They don't make sense. They have you behaving in ways that defy logical explanation. Smoking is a conspicuous example of this characteristic. It's a messy, unhealthy habit that leaves behind foul–smelling breath and clothing. It's expensive, and it will, in a variety of ways, according to mounds of medical research, ruin health and shorten life. Yet millions of people continue to puff cigarettes.

Strongholds are most often uncontrollable. If you have some type of behavior that seems to be handling you, rather than you handling it, you have a stronghold. It may be anger, drinking, eating, lying, lustful thoughts or feeling depressed. Whatever it is, you find it often getting the better of you, no matter how firmly you resolve not to let that happen.

Strongholds are counterproductive. This is perhaps the most invariable characteristic of Satan's works. They don't "work." They are strategies he has given us to use in coping with life's frustrations, but they only cause more problems. Classic examples are drugs and alcohol. Turning to these chemicals for "escape" only leads to a captivity that is more cruel and powerful than the ones we are trying to get away from.

The Lord revealed this design to a counselor who had spent several sessions with a mother whose stronghold was an obsessive fear of harming her own children. Over a period of weeks they prayed for God's power to bring down this stronghold, but it hadn't budged. Before the session began, they prayed for God to identify the barriers to victory and to remove them. As they shared, the Lord answered that prayer a bit at a time.

The design of the stronghold, as it unfolded in that session, revealed it to be not just a single structure but a hardened complex. It resembles Texas' famous Alamo, a fort standing within protective walls. The three basic elements of this fortification, all mentioned by Apostle Paul in 2 Corinthians 10, are:

1. The stronghold itself

    In this case, the central fortress was the woman's fear. This installation (to use another military analogy) is not simply a fortress but a fortified prison or dungeon. Within its granite walls, your thought patterns and emotional patterns pertaining to certain life experiences are held captive.

Through God's supernatural fire power, these dungeons can be leveled and every thought set free to follow Christ.

2. An inner wall or barricade — "imaginations"
    Surrounding the stronghold and protecting it against the attack was a wall the counselor had not seen before. As she talked about her problem, the woman said, "I don't know why I can't figure this thing out. I've tried to make sense of it, but the more I think about it, the more confused I become."

The Lord opened the counselor's eyes in that instant to what Paul meant when he referred to "imaginations." In various translations, the term is "reasonings," "arguments" and "rationalizations." The counselor saw that the main stronghold was not falling because she was still trying to work through the problem with human ability — by rationalizing, by seeking to understand it. The habitual tendency to rely on our own mental resources to deal with problems had become a wall of protection, warding off our attacks against the stronghold.

Psychological weapons are totally ineffective against strongholds, which have been constructed with spiritual power. The resources with which they were built are supernatural. They will not yield to mere natural weapons, however vigorously we wield them.

So, the counselor and counselee both realized that to get to the stronghold, this protective wall would first have to be breached. In order to do this, the mother would have to make a firm commitment to lay aside her own understanding and trust wholly in God's wisdom.

3. An outer wall or barricade — "high thing"

Later in the session, the woman said one of her fears had been that her Christian friends would find out about her problem and then think less of her. "They all think I'm a strong Christian," she said.

"Why does it bother you that they might discover you have problems?" the counselor asked. "Doesn't the Bible say we are to bear one another's burdens?"

"Oh, I guess it's just pride," she said. With that word, the Holy Spirit enlightened the counselor concerning another important truth shared by Paul in 2 Corinthians 10:5 concerning the design of strongholds: "Every high thing that exalteth itself against the knowledge of God" (KJV). Some translators render that phrase "proud thing."

Suddenly, it stood out clearly, as though the counselor were studying the enemy installation on an aerial photograph. Another wall surrounded the inner wall and protected the entire establishment. This wall was the wall of pride. The original language has also been translated "imposing thing" or "lofty thing." In light of the military analogy Paul makes throughout the passage, he undoubtedly meant to depict a high, imposing defensive wall built up to resist the knowledge of God. At the same time, he is using the phrase as a metaphor to denote pride or arrogance. An imposing barricade surrounding a military installation is a proud, defiant structure.

From this revelation, both saw that the great wall of pride would have to be shattered before the stronghold of fear could be destroyed. This would require her to ask God to do whatever might be necessary to destroy the stronghold — even if it involved embarrassment or humiliation for her. She would have to be like a soldier in war calling for an air strike while knowing the bombs might fall on him.

To review what God revealed in the "briefing" concerning the design of the stronghold:

Each stronghold is surrounded and protected by two walls — an inner wall of "imaginations" (rationalization, human reasoning) and an outer wall of "high things" (pride).

Attack Strategy

To attack a stronghold, then, we must have a good strategy. Rarely can we aim directly at the stronghold itself. We must first breach the outer wall of pride, then penetrate the inner wall of human mental effort — the tendency to try to figure things out within our own understanding.

For our attack to be successful, we must use the proper weapons. What are these weapons? Paul doesn't list them in these verses, but from other passages in both the Old and New Testaments, we know that the "heavy artillery" is the Word . . .

> *God wants to give us victory, but He can only do it if we show up for the battle.*

the truth . . . the power of God (2 Corinthians 6:7). God promises to cause His Word to triumph in everything He purposes for it (Jeremiah 1:12, Isaiah 55:11).

The second weapon might be seen as our own words, the prayers we speak or the commands we give to activate the Word of God. Jesus said, in John 16:24, "Hitherto have ye asked nothing in my name: ask, and ye shall receive, that your joy may be full" (KJV). The word "ask" in that verse has been translated "demand" or "command" by some translators. "Command" would be in keeping with the military analogy. A paraphrase of Jesus' words, in light of this analogy, could read something like this: "Until now, you haven't issued any commands in my name. Start issuing commands, and they shall be carried out, so that you can experience the joy of total victory."

As recipients of "The Great Commission," (Matthew 28:18–20), we are "commissioned officers" in God's army. We have not only the power and authority, but the duty to issue orders for attacks against the enemy strongholds. Jesus, the supreme commander, came to destroy the works of the devil (1 John 3:8), and we are the "troops" He has chosen to carry out that "seek and destroy" mission.

Commitment to Battle

Now that our strategy is clear and our weapons are ready, only one element of preparation remains to be carried out. We must commit ourselves to the battle. Remember, God wants to give us victory, but He can only do it if we show up for the battle.

God has always called on His commanders to confront the enemy. God told Jehoshaphat, " 'Be not afraid nor dismayed by reason of this great multitude [the Ammonites and Moabites who were attacking Jerusalem]; for the battle is not yours, but God's.' " And in the next breath He said, " 'To morrow go ye down against them . . . ' " (2 Chronicles 20:15–16 KJV).

Although the king was not going to do the fighting, he still had to present himself against the enemy. Moses had to confront Pharaoh, Gideon the Midianites, David the Philistines. Their firepower didn't win the victories. They were commanded to present themselves at the conflict. Even in the 2 Corinthians text, Paul says, "I beseech you, that I may not be bold against some . . . " (KJV). If a siege became necessary, Paul fully intended to be on the scene and available to wield his weapons by the power of God.

In order to follow this principle in a siege against a stronghold, we simply need to make ourselves available to be used in any way God directs. This is true whether the stronghold is in our own minds or those of others. We present ourselves on the battlefield, confront the enemy fortress and then remember God's words to Jehoshaphat: " 'Ye shall not need to fight . . . set yourselves . . . stand . . . and see the salvation of the Lord with you . . . ' " (2 Chronicles 20:17 KJV).

It is often necessary to find someone you can confide in, to share your heart and confess the reality of the stronghold you seek to tear down. Confession and humility releases healing power to restore us to wholeness. There is also great power in the prayer of agreement.

Ordering the Attack

To order an attack against a stronghold, we should pray in full recognition of who we are, our authority in Christ and the invincible power of our weapons. Above all, we must remember that we are operating in righteousness — a gift from God, through faith, to all who believe in Christ. A prayer launching an offensive against a stronghold, based on the strategy we have discussed, might sound something like this:

"Father, thank You for giving me Your righteousness in Christ, making me Your child and sharing your very nature with me. Thank You for giving me all power and authority because of my position in Christ and for commissioning me to wage spiritual warfare in Jesus' name. Now, Father, I command that this stronghold (identify it by name or description,) be brought down by your mighty weapons.

"First, to breach the wall of pride, I command the use of whatever weapons necessary to bring it down. Second, I command that the inner wall of "imaginations" or rationalizations be destroyed by neutralizing all human mental devices, so that there will be total dependence upon Your supernatural weapons. Finally, I command that the stronghold itself be destroyed and every thought be led out of Satan's bondage and into freedom with Christ. Thank You, Father, for the authority to issue these commands. I choose to believe they are being carried out and that You will deliver the victory You have promised. I make myself available to You for any use You see fit. Thank You for the victory in Jesus name. Amen.

The Victory Celebration

The victory celebration should begin immediately. In 2 Corinthians 2:14, we are told God is causing us to march in a continual victory parade in Christ. Jesus has already crushed Satan and all his power: "And having spoiled principalities and powers, he made a shew of them openly, triumphing over them in it" (Colossians 2:15 KJV). Because we are in Christ, that victory is ours. We can celebrate it and rest in the knowledge that it has been won.

Chapter
FIVE
Victory, Peace and Freedom

Victory, the Gift for Rejoicing

Many Christians hold a crippling misconception concerning spiritual warfare. They view it as an endless struggle. They see themselves almost as conscripted soldiers, chained to their weapons and destined to grapple wearily with their loathsome enemy throughout their days in this world.

To see our spiritual warfare in that light is to step into another of Satan's subtle traps. He likes nothing better than to see us working, struggling, toiling. He knows that work — any kind of work — produces fatigue, and when we are weary, we grow weak and give up. If we are making work of our spiritual privileges of prayer, Bible reading and witnessing, Satan sits back and waits for us to crumble under the burden. If we make a struggle of spiritual warfare, he watches with glee when we flail ourselves into exhaustion. He will even give us demons to chase about the landscape to hasten the tiring process.

> *Many Christians hold a crippling misconception concerning spiritual warfare. They view it as an endless struggle.*

You can avoid this pitfall if you understand that spiritual warfare differs markedly from human warfare. Jesus said, "Peace I give to you; not as the world gives do I give to you" (John 14:27 NASB).

When we fight His battles, we do not fight a human war. In the world, armies fight from positions of uncertainty toward the victory they hope to achieve after a painful and grueling struggle. The world's warfare is a fight where the participants battle without a confident knowledge of the outcome. But none of this is true of spiritual warfare. The army of believers does not struggle in the hope of achieving victory. We fight from the position of knowledge that the victory has already been won. The Christian's war is not a fight of works. It is a fight of faith (1 Timothy 6:12).

"Thanks be to God, who gives us the victory though our Lord Jesus Christ," Paul said (1 Corinthians 15:57 NASB). If God gives us the victory, then it must be His to give. For that to be so, it has to have already been won. And that is exactly the case. Colossians 2:15 tells us how complete the victory is that Jesus has won and handed to us: "When He had disarmed the rulers and authorities, He made a public display of them, having triumphed over them" (NASB).

By His death on the cross and subsequent resurrection, Jesus did not simply defeat the forces of darkness — He devastated them. The victory He won and handed to us is total, absolute. Jesus alluded to the thoroughness of the victory in Luke 10:18. His disciples have just returned from their mission of preaching the gospel, healing the sick and casting out demons in Jesus' name. Jesus responds to their breathless report with this rather bland remark: " 'I was watching Satan fall from heaven like lightning' " (NASB).

His words have been interpreted in several ways, but considering Jesus' eternal perspective, He seems to be saying He had already seen Satan utterly crushed by His victory on the cross. That victory is God's triumph over Lucifer and the angels who joined him in rebellion against God.

The chief point, regardless of the time element, is that Satan was not just pitched out of heaven and allowed to float softly down like a falling leaf. He was slammed down with the force of a bolt of lightning! He was utterly destroyed.

Since the complete victory already has been won, the warfare involves no struggle for us. Our fight is the "good fight of faith." Faith means simply believing what God has said and standing on that belief.

Our fight, then, is only in resisting the temptation to believe what the world, Satan and false doctrines say about spiritual warfare and choosing to believe what God says. And what does God say? Essentially what He said to Jehoshaphat when the enemy hordes descended on Jerusalem: " 'The battle is not yours but God's . . . You need not fight in this battle; station yourselves, stand and see the salvation of the Lord on your behalf' " (2 Chronicles 20:15–17 NASB).

Jesus said, "Be of good cheer; I have overcome the world" (John 16:33 KJV). That is past tense. It has been done. Since we are in Him and are one with Him, we have overcome. If it has been done, past tense, no struggle remains for us. It remains only for us to believe.

In Christ, we have been seated in the heavenly positions, far above all authority and power and dominion (Ephesians 1:21, 2:6), but Hebrews 2–4 gives us a further perspective on this truth.

Beginning with 2:8, the author reminds us that God gave man authority over all things and put all things under his feet. But now, he says, we do not see all things subjected to him. However, Christ came, identified Himself with man and, through death, destroyed the enemy. So, though we do not see all things subject to man, we can "consider Jesus" (3:1). He has put all things under His feet and, being "partakers of a heavenly calling" (NASB), we can take His victory as ours the moment we believe and receive it. Then, in Him, we have all things under our feet!

He has won the victory and given it to us. Like any gift, the gift of victory leaves us with only two options. We cannot achieve it; we can only reject it or receive it.

Since Christ has already given us the victory, our role in

combat is quite different from that of the soldier in human warfare. We present ourselves at the battlefield and confront the enemy, as Jehoshaphat was instructed to do. We call in God's power and issue commands in Jesus' name to the heavenly hosts, as Elisha did when he was surrounded at Dothan (2 Kings 6:18). But

> *We celebrate the victory — even while the battle rages!*

we do not fight. We celebrate the victory — even while the battle rages! We sing and praise God for loving us and for giving us His power over the enemy, as Jehoshaphat's people did when Jerusalem was besieged (2 Chronicles 20:18–22).

In 2 Corinthians 2:14, Paul paints an exciting picture of the company of believers engaged in spiritual warfare: "Thanks be to God, who always leads us in triumph in Christ, and manifests through us the sweet aroma of the knowledge of Him in every place" (NASB). These phrases do not depict a smoky, bloody, sweaty battlefield littered with worn-out, wounded and broken bodies. They picture a joyous victory parade.

Paul drew the analogy from the customs of the Roman culture in which he lived. When a Roman army won a major victory, the conquering heroes received a gala welcome on their return to the city. The commander led the column, followed by all the troops who had contributed to the battle. Behind them, bound in chains and rendered utterly harmless, limped the vanquished enemy. The sweet fragrance of the victorious warriors' incense wafted through the cheering crowds that lined the parade route. The crowds responded by tossing garlands and bouquets on the victors. It was a moment of great glory and exultation.

For the Christian in spiritual warfare, though, the celebration will not be fleeting; it will be constant. According to Paul, God always leads us in this victory parade. Christ leads the column. We march behind, trailed by the enemy whom we have bound and incapacitated — the evidence of our victory. The incense we carry is the knowledge of Christ — the fact that we know Him personally, that we rely on Him, and that in Him we are continuously victorious.

Once you see this scene, you begin to understand why people do not swarm to our churches to hear about Christ today. They do not see the victory parade. They see too much struggle, fatigue, pain and defeat.

It is the sweet fragrance of victory and the knowledge that victory comes only through Christ that draws the multitudes to Jesus, not human persuasion or evangelistic programs. When we invite the crowds to a victory, they will come to Christ in droves, just as they did in the early days of the Church.

Confront the enemy. Receive the victory by faith, instead of trying to achieve it by works. Celebrate, marching triumphantly in the victory parade. Then you will know the joy of successful spiritual warfare.

Peace: The Gift for Resting

In Philippians 4:7, Paul tells us that for the believer there is a peace that "surpasses all comprehension." It is beyond the grasp of the human understanding. Mere men cannot fathom it with all their powers of logic.

Again, Paul uses a military analogy to help us understand how important this peace is to the Christian in spiritual combat. It "will guard your hearts and your minds in Christ Jesus" (NASB), he says.

You can rejoice in the peace God gives you, but He has not given it simply for you to enjoy. It serves an important purpose for you in spiritual combat. This peace guards your heart and your mind. If God gives you a peace to guard your heart and mind, we must assume that they need to be guarded. The scriptures do not identify the dangers in this passage, but we can make some educated guesses.

Threats aimed at the mind could include doubt, fear or false information fed to you by the enemy concerning the battlefield situation, your strategies, your firepower or the very nature of spiritual warfare. As previously noted, Satan constantly tries to deceive us into making a struggle of spiritual warfare. When we receive the peace of God, that satanic plot is one of the major dangers from which the peace guards our minds.

But Satan can also attack our hearts. The heart is our spirit, our new nature in Christ. It is what we are, our identity. If Satan can get us confused about who we are at any point in spiritual warfare, he has undermined our power over him.

Perhaps this is why Jesus warned His disciples when they returned from their preaching, healing, delivering mission not to rejoice that the demons were subject to them in His name, but that their own names were written in heaven (Luke 10: 17–20). In other words, in the excitement of victory, never forget who you are. Never forget that it is by virtue of your identity as a child of God that you wield this unlimited power over the enemy. Rejoice in the fact that you have a personal and eternal relationship with the living God. Never forget who you are, where you derive your power from and the real reason for the war — the glory of the Lord Jesus Christ; that would invite defeat in the next encounter. The peace of God guards your heart against that pitfall.

The term "peace" presupposes that there has been a battle and the result is complete victory. The enemy has been defeated, all resistance has been crushed and hostilities have ceased. As a spiritual warrior, Christ has won the victory, and God has given it to you. In the same way, He gives you peace. It is a gift of God.

When the angel proclaimed the birth of the Messiah to the shepherds, the benediction was a chorus of the heavenly host, praising God and saying, " . . . on earth peace" (Luke 2:14). The good news preached by Jesus and the apostles was a "gospel of peace" (Ephesians 6:15). Jesus said, "Peace I leave with you; My peace I give to you; not as the world gives do I give to you" (John 14:27 NASB). In sending Christ into the world, God's primary purpose was to establish peace by conquering the enemy and to give that peace to us!

The verse just quoted contains two clues as to why the peace of God surpasses human understanding. First, it is Christ's peace. That means divine peace, a supernatural thing (1 Corinthians 2:9–14). Secondly, it is "not as the world gives." The worldly mind is conditioned to understand a certain kind of peace, which keeps us from understanding God's peace.

However, it is important for us as believers to understand the peace of God to a degree.

First, we must bear in mind that God's peace differs from the world's peace. It does not depend on sense–knowledge evidence to confirm it. You have, and can experience, the peace of God when your visible circumstances bring sheer turmoil. Your peace is "of

God," which means it emanates from the invisible, spiritual realm. You experience it in the "inner man," not necessarily externally. To experience peace, the world has to see the enemy vanquished and the surrender flag waving over his fortifications, but your peace is "by faith, not by sight" (2 Corinthians 5:7). Outwardly,

> *Never forget that it is by virtue of your identity as a child of God that you wield this unlimited power over the enemy.*

you may still be in the throes of bitter conflict. You may yet be the target of fierce enemy fire. Your situation may seem hopeless to any bystanders, but in the midst of the outer chaos, you enjoy the most wonderful peace. Why? Because you are not looking at the things that are seen (2 Corinthians 4:18). You are looking at God's version of reality, not the world's. You have chosen to believe what the Lord says about the situation, not the false communiqués of the enemy, designed to dishearten and disarm you.

You are not trying to achieve peace by fighting for victory. You have chosen to receive peace by believing the Word of God — His assurance that Christ has already won the victory and that He has given it to you.

The second thing to remember about the peace of God is that, like the victory He gives you, it is total and complete. It is not like the peace we often see in the world, which is actually an armed truce. The enemy is not regrouping, setting up ambushes and waiting stealthily for an opportunity to strike again. Externally, that may seem to be the case, but in the spiritual realm of reality, the victory and the peace are absolute. In His work on the cross, Jesus destroyed "him who had the power of death, that is, the devil" (Hebrews 2:14 NASB).

This sheds light on the words of John: "For whatever is born of God overcomes the world; and this is the victory that has overcome the world — our faith" (1 John 5:4 NASB). The victory that establishes peace for us has already been won. By faith — by believing that to be true — we bring that victory, and that peace, into reality for ourselves.

The faith requirement is revealed in Philippians 4:6, the verse preceding God's promise of peace. It reads: "Be anxious for nothing, but in everything by prayer and supplication with thanksgiving let your requests be made known to God" (NASB). In everything, call for the power and provision of God — then trust Him with it. That is faith. That is what releases the peace of God to you to guard your heart and mind.

The guard is quite adequate and secure. The word "guard," sometimes rendered "garrison," suggests not just a lone sentry but an entire occupation force of the heavenly host! Under the protection of such power, you can indeed be "anxious for nothing."

The King James version of Isaiah 26:3 presents another picture of the military analogy. "Thou wilt keep him in perfect peace, whose mind is stayed on thee: because he trusteth in thee (KJV)."

Set your mind on the Lord and His promises, trust in Him and you will experience "perfect peace." Not peace as the world gives, but a perfect peace. And God will keep you in that state of peace. Again, the word "keep" suggests a garrison, a large military force, stationed about you to repulse any enemy attack.

Finally, we must understand that, though the enemy may still exist around your perimeters, the peace of God produces periods of relief from attacks of harassment. The enemy would like you to think there is no rest. He wants you to become weary just thinking about the warfare. If he can misguide you into believing that you will have him to reckon with every waking moment for as long as you live, he can undermine your will to confront him.

After Jesus had His encounter with Satan just after the baptism, Satan left Him, and angels ministered to Him. He did not have to fight the devil with every step He took.

James said, "Submit therefore to God. Resist the devil and he will flee from you" (James 4:7 NASB). Satan may return, but he loses his stomach for battle for a season when you have overcome him in the power of the Spirit.

The Old Testament records many instances in which God's people enjoyed periods of freedom from harassment after victories over their enemies.

— After Gideon and his 300 defeated the Midianites, "Midian was subdued before the sons of Israel, and they did not lift up their heads anymore. And the land was undisturbed for forty years in the days of Gideon" (Judges 8:28 NASB).

— After Jehoshaphat's victory over the sons of Ammon, Moab and Mount Seir, "The kingdom of Jehoshaphat was at peace, for his God gave him rest on all sides" (2 Chronicles 20:30 NASB).

The last verse is particularly revealing. It underscores the fact that it is God who gives the peace. It also links peace and rest. When we believe that Christ has won the victory for us and we have received it by faith, the peace that follows is a rest. Hebrews 4:9–10 presents this rest as a permanent condition in which believers are to abide: "There remaineth therefore a rest to

In everything, call for the power and provision of God — then trust Him with it.

the people of God. For he that is entered into his rest, he also hath ceased from his own works, as God did from his" (KJV).

The peace of God surpasses all comprehension. It is simply too wonderful for the human mind to grasp. But it is essential to our success in spiritual warfare, and God has given it to us. There is nothing left for us to do but receive it by faith and rest!

Freedom: The Gift for Restoration

Sometimes, in our preoccupation with the battles at hand, we lose sight of the purpose of our warfare. We tend to think of nothing but destroying the enemy and of guarding against his sneak attacks and harassment. Or we get caught up in celebration of the victory and peace we have received and never go on to appropriate what that victory and peace have purchased for us.

The ultimate purpose of our spiritual warfare is freedom — freedom from everything that has bound us and prevented us from being fulfilled in all God intended us to be as His creations.

In announcing His mission in the world, Jesus quoted an Old Testament messianic prophecy from Isaiah 61:1, which included the phrase "to proclaim liberty to the captives" (KJV). That is central to His purpose. Who are the captives? All who have been held in slavery by Satan.

Ephesians 1:7 says that we have redemption through the blood of Jesus. To redeem is to set free, as slaves were freed in Jesus' day when someone paid their owner the price for their release. When Jesus paid the price for our sins, He redeemed us. He set us free. The writer of Hebrews leads us to see that God has included all believers in the liberating mission of Christ. Hebrews 2:14–15 tells us that Jesus came to destroy the devil and "free those who through fear of death were subject to slavery all their lives " (NASB). That is the basic objective of spiritual warfare — to "deliver" those who have been held in slavery because of the fear of death.

Then Hebrews 3:1 says: "Therefore, holy brethren, partakers of a heavenly calling, consider Jesus, the Apostle and High Priest of our confession" (NASB). All who believe in Christ are members of the holy brotherhood, of which Jesus is the High Priest. All are partakers of His heavenly calling. The "therefore" at the be ginning of the verse gives us the clue to the identification of that calling. It is the same calling Jesus had in the previous chapter — to destroy the devil and deliver the captives. We are to see ourselves as champions of liberty, though even freedom is not an end in itself. Freedom is granted to serve a heavenly purpose, but most believers do not think of it that way. This is evidenced by the fact that, in discussing our freedom, we talk almost exclusively about what we are free from.

What we are free from does make exciting praise material. We are free from the wrath of God, from the law, from the penalty of sin, from the elementary principles of the world, from the traditions of men, from the dominion of sin, from the bondage to the forces of darkness. The list goes on and on. Jesus said, "If the Son therefore shall make you free, ye shall be free indeed," (John 8:36 KJV). "Indeed" means totally, absolutely free. What a marvelous truth! Little wonder that we focus so much attention on all that we are free from.

But Colossians 1:13 says, "For He rescued us from the domain of darkness, and transferred us to the kingdom of His beloved Son" (NASB). Note the dual aspect of our deliverance. God did not just deliver us from something; He also delivered us to something. He delivered us from the domain or rule of darkness, but He also transferred us to the kingdom of God — the kingdom ruled by Jesus Christ, the King of kings!

Now that we have been freed from the kingdom of darkness, and all the bondage to which we were subject in that domain, and transferred to the kingdom of God, it is time that we devoted less attention to what we have been delivered from and more attention to what we have been delivered to. It is time to concentrate less on what we have been set free from and more on what we have been set free for.

When the American colonies won their independence from England, they were set free from many evils — unjust taxation, arbitrary violations of civil liberties, military conscription, confiscation of private property, and rule by a distant, unresponsive, legislative dictatorship. But once the cord to Britain was cut, citizens of the new nation did not simply sit around and celebrate all the things they had been set free from. They changed their focus to the things they had been set free for. They began to exercise their freedom to seek the individual fulfillment and national development that had been denied them as subjects of the Crown. They began to take advantage of the "inalienable rights" they had fought to secure — the right to life, liberty and the pursuit of happiness.

If that course of action in the political realm produced the wealthiest and most powerful nation in history, what could it produce in the spiritual realm? When America brandishes its power, the world trembles. How much more would the gates of Hell shake at a genuine manifestation of the power of the Kingdom of God!

What are the things for which we have been set free? It would be folly to attempt a complete list. There are few verses in the

Bible, especially in the New Testament, that do not contain some power, privilege or prerogative relating to the provision for the exercise of our freedom.

The word that sums up all that we have been set free for, of course, is life. We tend to take that word lightly, but the Lord's discourse on life — the meaning and importance of it — occupies a great proportion of the Scriptures, including most of the Gospel of John. He makes it clear that life is possessed only by God and those to whom He gives it (John 5:21–26), and He gives it only to those who believe in Him and receive it by faith (John 6:47). It is eternal life; it is God's own life — abundant, fulfilled, overflowing (John 10:10b).

More of the lost masses would be drawn to Christ if Christians simply realized their freedom to relax and live. Because so many of us have been drawn back into bondage to some of the things we have been freed from, the unsaved rarely see an example of the abundant life. They turn from the misery, bondage and defeat they witness in the Church, because it does not appear to be any better than what they already experience. In fact, it can seem more oppressing! This may explain Paul's frequent warnings for believers to beware of being lured back

> *The word that sums up all that we have been set free for, of course, is life.*

into slavery after having been set free.

"See to it that no one takes you captive through philosophy and empty deception, according to the tradition of men, according to the elementary principles of the world, rather than according to Christ" (Colossians 2:8 NASB).

"Philosophy" and "elementary principles" are the beliefs, customs and traditions in which we are brought up in the world. It is appalling, the extent to which many of the most active Christians allow their lives to be controlled by the things of human culture — everything from sayings and axioms, to old wives' tales and "folk knowledge" passed down through the generations. We have been freed from the bonds of these things. We are free to enjoy the principles of the Kingdom of God. That means living life by faith and not by works, trusting rather than trying, resting rather than wrestling.

"He who has the Son has the life" (1 John 5:12 NASB). We have been set free to live. Let's get on with it!

As believers born again into God's family, we also have the blessed privilege of entering into His presence. Hebrews 10:19 reveals that we have been granted this privilege through the blood of Jesus, and we are encouraged to use it.

Because of this privilege, we are free to enjoy fellowship with our heavenly Father and with His Son any time we desire (1 John

1:3). But how often do we exercise that privilege? When we open the Word, how often is it simply to bask in the presence of God and the Lord Jesus, rather than to find some rule to follow or some scripture to bolster our arguments or doctrinal positions? How often do we simply sit in some quiet place and glory in the fact that God has invited us into His presence?

However, our being in His presence also has a divine purpose. We are to exercise this freedom in order to receive mercy and find grace in times of need (Hebrews 4:16).

Most of us see this as an invitation to run to the Lord every time we have consciousness of a sin to get mercy and grace for ourselves, and our freedom to enter His presence does serve that purpose. From our positions of acceptance and holiness before God, though, we should see this freedom serving a far greater purpose in the Kingdom of God. It is our privilege to go with confidence to the throne of grace to receive mercy and grace for others in their times of need.

That brings us to another neglected aspect of our freedom — our freedom to minister to others. Now that we are free from laboring to fulfill the law, obey the rules and avoid the punishment that bound us, we are free to switch our attention from ourselves to the unsaved and to fellow believers who are in need of our help. Our power and resources for this ministry are truly awesome.

The first to be mentioned is one rarely used in the Church today — the power to forgive sins. In John 20:23, Jesus says, "If you forgive the sins of any, their sins have been forgiven them; if you retain the sins of any, they have been retained" (NASB).

The implications of that delegation of authority are simply mind–boggling. How much more effective might our evangelism be if we went to sinners as Jesus did, not detailing a list of their sins and the dread consequences to them, but saying, "Your sins are forgiven" (NASB). Jesus never discussed the sins of those He saved, healed and delivered except to say, "I do not condemn you" (John 8:11 NASB). The only ones He forced to face their sins were the self-righteous who tried to deny they had sins.

In Christ, we are free to serve others though His power and provision.

How many more might rise, take up their beds and walk if we ministered forgiveness to them? This is a vital purpose of our freedom in Christ — forgiving others as God in Christ has forgiven us (Ephesians 4:32).

Without even citing Scripture references, many of us could tick off a long list of ways to fulfill the purpose of our freedom in ministry to others: through deliverance from demonic control or harassment, by healing, by comforting, by teaching, by encouraging, by interceding to appropriate God's provision, by bearing burdens, by sharing and giving to meet needs of every description, by simply expressing our love.

This is not a task; it is a privilege. It is not a law or require ment to drag us back into bondage; it is an exercise of our freedom. Before, we were in bondage to the necessity of trying to serve ourselves. In Christ, we are free to serve others though His power and provision!

Finally, another great purpose of our freedom is one that people often ignore to avoid sounding selfish: our personal fulfillment.

What makes us shy away from this purpose of our freedom is a false modesty that is actually part of the bondage from which Christ has liberated us. We are new creations, His workmanship (2 Corinthians 5:17, Ephesians 2:10).

He has given us individuality. He intends us to be fulfilled in all that He created and ordained us to be.

We are free to pursue that fulfillment. Since Christ is all in all to us, one of the major freedoms we have is freedom from self-consciousness, which produces false modesty, guilt and other bondages detrimental to our fulfillment.

God has promised to satisfy the desire of every living thing (Psalm 145:16). In case we might not understand that "living things" include His own beloved children, He gave Paul the word we find in Romans 8:32: "He who did not spare His own Son, but delivered Him over for us all, how will He not also with Him freely give us all things?" (NASB).

He has promised to give us the desires of our hearts (Psalm 37:4) and to provide, through the gifts and ministries of others, for us to attain to the status of "a mature man, to the measure of the stature which belongs to the fullness of Christ" (Ephesians 4:13 NASB).

If Christ attained His potential to be fulfilled in all He was meant to be, then, according to this verse, God desires and expects us to be fulfilled.

In His parable of the sheepfold, Jesus said: " 'I am the door; if anyone enters through Me, he will be saved, and will go in and out and find pasture' " (John 10:9 NASB).

What an exhilarating picture of the results of successful spiritual warfare: the enemy has been engaged, the victory won and peace established. Now the "sheep" are free to go in and out and find pasture — personal fulfillment, the abundant life — without being burdened by the chains of their former captor or fear of assault or harassment. Through His triumph over Satan, our Lord Jesus, the Captain of our host, has prepared a table before us in the presence of our enemies!

Acts 3:19–21 presents the overall purpose of the freedom God has given us through Christ:

"Therefore repent and return, so that your sins may be wiped away, in order that times of refreshing may come from the presence of the Lord; and that He may send Jesus, the Christ appointed for you, whom heaven must receive until the period of restoration of all things about which God spoke by the mouth of His holy prophets from ancient time" (NASB).

The purpose of our freedom is great: having received victory and peace with God through Jesus, whom He sent to save us, we have been set free and brought into God's presence. There we rest and receive mercy and grace for ministering the life of Christ to others. That ministry, the ultimate purpose of our freedom, is the "restoration of all things" — the returning to the Church the blessings, unity, authority, power and glory God ordained for it to display.

What a glorious purpose! This is what God has given us in Christ. You are not fighting and waiting for some magnificent day, who knows how far in the future, when you will at last experience victory, peace and freedom. You have them now! You can rejoice in them, even while the battle continues in the visible realm. That is how God has provided for you to enjoy the love, power and blessings of the life of Jesus in the world.

Chapter SIX

Your Heart's Desire

Your Heart's Desire

What do you want in life? What do you really want? You may be among the many Christians who have never answered that question for themselves. Or you may be among those who know what you want but find it a source of frustration and confusion. Somewhere along the way, you have picked up the idea that it is selfish for you to want something, that anything you might want is contrary to the will of God for your life.

What a tragedy that so many Christians spend their lives in emptiness and misery because of this grotesque misconception! The things you want, those desires that cry out from your innermost being, are not contrary to the will of God for you, if you are a Christian; they constitute the primary means by which God reveals His will for you. This may seem a strange subject to include under "spiritual warfare," but confusion on this point leads to some of the worst defeats Christians suffer.

The word "desire" got its bad reputation when we started associating it with "desires of the flesh," those self–centered desires that were part of the old Adamic nature we had before we received Christ as Savior and were crucified with Him (Romans 6:6). Speaking to born–again believers in Ephesians 2:3, Paul makes it clear that Christians no longer pursue those self–serving desires. "We too all formerly lived in the lusts of our flesh, indulging the desires of the flesh and of the mind" (NASB), he said. In the unsaved person, "the flesh" is the Adamic nature, the corrupted spirit of man, the sin–defiled heart. The desires of that wicked heart overwhelm and poison the mind as well, but Paul emphasizes that this is the walk of Christians before they are saved. When the unsaved receive Christ as Savior, they receive a heart transplant, as was prophesied in Ezekiel 36:26: "Moreover, I will give you a new heart and put a new spirit within you; and I will remove the heart of stone from your flesh and give you a heart of flesh" (NASB). Paul put it another way in 2 Corinthians 5:17–18: "Therefore if anyone is in Christ, he is a new creature; the old things have passed away; behold, new things have come. Now all things are from God" (NASB).

Now notice the exciting truths this reveals:

1. When we received Christ, we became new creations.
2. In our new state, all things are from God, who did the work of the new creation (Ephesians 2:10).
3. The new heart we have, then, is from God, and everything in it was put there by Him.
4. The "all things new," then, include the desires of our hearts.

Since the desires of our hearts are from God, how could they be self–centered, sinful and contrary to His will? They could not be, of course. Rather, they were placed in our hearts, like the internal guidance mechanism inside a missile, to aim us in the direction in which God wants us to go. Our desires are inseparable from what we are and what God wants us to do. We are the will of God: "Born, not of blood nor of the will of the flesh nor of the will of man, but of God" (John 1:13 NASB). And the desires of our hearts are but reflections of what we are.

> *God promises not just to "meet our needs," but to give us the desires of our hearts as well.*

Now we can rejoice in the desires of our hearts, those things we really want in life. We can thank God for them. We can rebuke Satan any time he tries to make us feel guilty or ashamed of them. They are a vital part of God's gift of Eternal Life to us and a means by which He can lead us where He wants us to go.

Seen in this light, many of God's promises, which make us uncomfortable in our ignorant false humility, take on new meaning. When we hear Jesus saying, "Ask, and it shall be given you" (Matthew 7:7 KJV), "If you ask Me anything in My name, I will do it" (John 14:14 NASB), "Ask whatever you wish, and it will be done for you" (John 15:7 NASB), what is our first impulse? Is it not to say, "But . . . it can't be something I want for myself. But . . . it must be 'according to the will of God.' But . . . if I really want it, I can't ask for it; that would be sinful"?

If we understand that God has made us new creations and given us a whole new set of desires, we can accept Jesus' instructions. When He said, "ask and it shall be given to you," "anything," "whatever you wish," He was not misstating Himself. He knew exactly what He was telling us to do. And He intended us to do just that, so that "your joy may be made full" (John 16:24 NASB).

God makes this conclusion abundantly clear in His Word. Psalm 37:4 says: "Delight yourself in the Lord; and He will give you the desires of your heart" (NASB).

It could hardly be said with greater clarity that God's will is for the desires of our hearts to be fulfilled, but the statement is reaffirmed in numerous verses.

Psalm 21:1–2 says: "Oh Lord, in Your strength the king will be glad, and in Your salvation how greatly he will rejoice! You have given him his heart's desire, and You have not withheld the request of his lips" (NASB).

The verbs are past tense, meaning it has, in the mind of God, already been done. We can see it in this light if we understand that all things are fulfilled for us in Christ. We have been established to reign in life (Romans 5:17), and we are "king-priests" and "queen-priestesses" as members of His "royal priesthood" (1 Peter 2:9). When the psalm speaks of "the king" (or queen), it speaks of all who are in Christ.

The intent of God to fulfill the desires of our hearts is revealed again in Proverbs 10:24: "What the wicked fears will come upon him, but the desire of the righteous will be granted" (NASB).

Notice how God promises not just to "meet our needs," but to give us the desires of our hearts as well. Many Christians, because they don't know their exalted position in Christ ("seated . . . with Him in the heavenly places . . . " Ephesians 2:6 NASB), pray to God as though He were a miserly tyrant instead of a loving Father. They ask only for their needs — the bare necessities of life. They are afraid they will offend by asking for the things they want. But God says our needs are already met, because we stand with Him in Christ (Matthew 6:33, Philippians 4:19). We can cease worrying about those and start trusting Him to fulfill our desires.

Through many passages, God reveals how unfair we are to Him and ourselves when we approach Him with a beggarly attitude.

In Psalm 145:16 we read: "You open Your hand and satisfy the desire of every living thing." So we will know that "every living thing" includes us, verse 19 says: "He will fulfill the desire of those who fear Him" (NASB).

Just in case His children have still missed the point, the Lord gives us Psalm 104:26–28: "There the ships move along, and Leviathan, which You have formed to sport in it. They wait for You to give them their food in due season. You give to them, they gather it up; You open Your hand, they are satisfied with good" (NASB).

The Leviathan is a sea creature, good for nothing but frolicking in the ocean. If God fulfills the desire of every living thing, including this seemingly worthless creature, will He not stand good in His promise to fulfill the hearts' desires of those who love Him?

Jesus confirms these promises in many other verses, including Mark 11:24: "Therefore I say to you, all things for which you pray and ask, believe that you have received them, and they will be granted you" (NASB).

Paul stresses the "all things" theme in Romans 8:32: "He who did not spare His own Son, but delivered Him up for us all, how will He not also with Him freely give us all things?" (NASB).

And again in 1 Corinthians 3:21–23: "So then let no one boast in men. For all things belong to you, whether Paul or Apollos or Cephas or the world or life or death or things present or things to come; all things belong to you, and you belong to Christ; and Christ belongs to God" (NASB).

Other verses make it clear that everything necessary for fulfilling the desires of our hearts has already been deeded over to us in Christ, and that now it is simply a matter of our recognizing the fact and applying these resources through faith.

Ephesians 1:3: "Blessed be the God and Father of our Lord Jesus Christ, who has blessed us with every spiritual blessing in the heavenly places in Christ" (NASB).

2 Peter 1:3: "His divine power has granted to us everything pertaining to life and godliness, through the true knowledge of Him who called us by His own glory and excellence" (NASB).

The Bible is full of examples of God fulfilling the hearts' desires of those who trust Him, but none is more dramatic than the case of Solomon, recorded in 1 Kings 3:1–13. The Lord appears to Solomon in a dream, in verse 5, and says: " 'Ask what you wish me to give you.' " Solomon tells the Lord the desire of his heart: " 'Give Your servant an understanding heart to judge Your people to discern between good and evil' " (Verse 9), and the Lord found this request pleasing. Then God simply grants the request without conditions or reservations: " 'Behold, I have done according to your words. Behold, I have given you a wise and discerning heart, so that there has been no one like you before you, nor shall one like you arise after you' " (Verse 12).

> *The Bible is full of examples of God fulfilling the hearts' desires of those who trust Him.*

In verse 13, however, the Lord reveals just how intent He is upon giving us the desires of our heart: " 'I have also given you what you have not asked, both riches and honor, so that there will not be any among the kings like you in all your days' " (NASB).

God saw Solomon's heart. He knew that Solomon desired

more than he had revealed. He perceived that Solomon desired to be a great king, not for himself but for the glory of the Lord. Perhaps Solomon had hesitated to ask out of false humility, fearing the Lord might think him arrogant or presumptuous. But God insisted on fulfilling the whole desire of Solomon's heart, even the part he had not dared to ask for!

That is how our loving Father deals with us, His children. If He can persuade us to ask for the tiniest desire of our heart, He will fulfill far beyond what we have asked (Ephesians 3:20: "[He] is able to do far more abundantly beyond all that we ask or think, according to the power that works within us" NASB). For His desire is to fulfill all of our desires.

The Source of Our Heart's Desire

One reason many believers refuse to ask God for their hearts' desires is that they are confused about the source of those desires. They are under the false impression that the desires originate from the world, "the flesh" or even the devil. That misconception stems from a failure to understand that when people receive Christ as Savior and are born again, they receive a new heart. With the new heart comes a new set of desires.

It helps us to understand this if we recognize that the heart, spirit and nature are all the same in scripture, and that they all refer to the core of our being. The heart, the spirit, the nature — this is what we are in our innermost personhood. This is our true identity, our basic character.

Thus, when God says in Ezekiel 36:26 that He will give those in Christ a new heart, or a new spirit, He is saying He will make them something entirely different from what they were before. He will change their very nature; He will give them a new identity.

When we realize this, Paul's words in the verses quoted earlier take on a literal meaning that some Christians never ascribe to them. We are "new creations," as he says in 2 Corinthians 5:17 (NIV). Old things have passed away; all things have become new. All things in this new creation are from God (Verse 18). We are His workmanship (Ephesians 2:10).

Therefore, whatever has gone into that new heart He gave us has come from Him, including the desires of that heart.

Why question whether He really means to fulfill those desires? If they are from Him, if He gave them to us when He created us anew in Christ, why wouldn't He want them to be fulfilled?

It also stands to reason that if He gave us the desires of our hearts He had some purpose in doing so. And what could that purpose be but to guide us into the activities and pursuits that constitute His specific will for our lives?

Ponder the implications of this. It means that many Christians, in hesitating to ask God to fulfill the desires of their hearts are thwarting His will for their lives, rather than pleasing Him. In doing so, they are displeasing Him and robbing themselves.

What are the Desires of Your Heart?

What sort of desires does God include in "the desires of your heart"? The answer is summarized in 2 Peter 1:3: "His divine power has granted to us everything pertaining to life and godliness" (NASB). In other words, a desire of the heart might involve anything in any way related to living in this world and walking in fellowship with God!

When considering the desires of our hearts, we tend to belittle material things — because Jesus said we are not to be anxious about such things — or to magnify them out of proportion of their true importance. Actually, the Lord gives us the correct perspective on the material. He said life is more than food and clothing (Matthew 6:25), and that we should not be preoccupied or worried about such things. But He acknowledged that we need them, assuring us that if we seek the rule of God in our lives, these things "will be added" (Verse 33 NASB).

Simple logic should tell us that material things are included in the hearts' desires God has promised to satisfy. If God gave you the spiritual gifts for a colossal ministry, but did not provide you with food, clothing, transportation and other material needs, what could you accomplish for Him?

Any gift from God is a spiritual gift, whether tangible or intangible, visible or invisible, large or small.

That brings us to another barrier that prevents many believers from having their hearts' desires fulfilled: the magnitude of the desire. Either they fear that a desire is too great to bring to the Lord, or they fear it is too small. But remember, He has given us everything that pertains to life and godliness.

"Nothing will be impossible with God" (Luke 1:37 NASB), so you should not be intimidated to ask God to fulfill the big desires. Sometimes, however, it seems that believers stumble less at asking for the big things than the small.

For example, a woman who had walked with the Lord for many years and allowed God to use her in a mighty way to minister to others had, since childhood, seen Him in the beauty of the natural creation around her. She loved trees, flowers, the blue skies, the rain, the sea. In the animal kingdom, her favorite creatures were the birds.

For many years she fed wild birds in her backyard during the winter. The cardinal, with its brilliant coloring and inspiring song, was her favorite bird. Although her feedings had attracted many species, she had never been visited by a redbird.

"I want a redbird so badly," she told her husband one day, "and

I've never had one."

"Have you ever asked the Lord for one?" he asked

"No, come to think of it. I haven't."

"Then I'm going to ask Him to send you one, and if you'll agree with me in prayer, I know you'll have one soon, because He has promised to fulfill the desires of your heart."

In a matter of two weeks, the woman peeked out her back window one morning to see a beautiful male cardinal perched in a tree above her bird feeders. She was still praising God for this marvelous answer to prayer two days later when she looked out again and saw a female cardinal eating from one of the feeders while the male bird observed from the tree.

> *Either we fear that a desire is too great to bring to the Lord, or we fear it is too small.*

God had answered her prayer beyond her fondest hopes. He had sent her a pair of cardinals to be permanent residents! She enjoyed the blessing of their presence morning and evening every day. She counted it as a token of God's boundless love that He would fulfill even such a small and unimportant desire!

Another heart's desire Christians sometimes find difficult to share with God concerns interpersonal relations. The devil tries to intimidate us by labeling such desires selfish, presumptuous or even lustful. But in our new creation, God designed us to be social beings. It follows that we have social needs and desires, like psychological, emotional and physical desires. Again, since God placed those desires in our hearts when He created us, they are among the desires He promised to fulfill.

In trusting the Lord to fulfill these social desires believers must be open to God's provision. He is not confined to human resources and logic or the traditions of men in meeting our needs. When He fulfilled Adam's social desires, it was simply because He saw that it was not good for the man to be alone (Genesis 2:18), but He did so in a manner that Adam probably never dreamed of — by putting him to sleep, taking a rib from his side and fashioning it into a woman. This was a total surprise to Adam, who apparently had thought he could find a "helper suitable for him" from among the creatures God had already made (Genesis 2:20 NASB). His response to God's solution reveals that he found it utterly satisfactory. Put in today's language, it would sound something like: "At last! This is what I've been longing for."

We should not be reluctant to pray for the right friends, the right mate, children and other persons through whom God may choose to fulfill our social desires.

One word of caution on the point, however: there is one thing God has chosen never to do, and that is to force His will upon an individual. He can, and does, work with people to woo them and persuade them through circumstances, knowledge and the call of the Holy Spirit. But He allows their will to remain sovereign. He won't even force anyone to come to Him; we can't expect Him to compel anyone to come to us.

In praying for God to fulfill our hearts' social desires, we must allow Him to be sovereign in the choice of the particular individuals involved. We cannot ask Him to use His divine power to control the life of another person for our benefit. He has that person's desires to respect and fulfill, also.

Finally, God's promise includes what most Christians classify as "spiritual" desires. These desires are primarily longings to be in the presence of God, to have communion with Him, to be aware of His love and acceptance for us, to walk in fellowship with Him. Christians should not find it hard to believe that these desires are from God and that He is eager to fulfill them, since He pleads with us throughout His Word to turn to Him and promises always to be there for us when we do: "I will never desert you, nor will I ever forsake you" (Hebrews 13:5 NASB).

One verse in particular gives emphasis to His desire to fulfill our spiritual desires: "What we have seen and heard we proclaim to you also, so that you too may have fellowship with us; and indeed our fellowship is with the Father, and with His Son Jesus Christ" (1 John 1:3 NASB).

We are to "draw near with confidence to the throne of grace" (Hebrews 4:16 NASB), knowing that our Father welcomes His children there with open arms.

Desires of the heart are not to be confused, of course, with "desires of the flesh." The distinguishing characteristic of the latter is that they are self–centered. They are calculated to serve selfish interests. And they are fulfilled by self–effort — with one's own human wisdom, strength and resources. God does not act to satisfy the desires of the flesh:

> *Desires of the heart are not to be confused, of course, with "desires of the flesh."*

"You were dead in your trespasses and sins, in which you formerly walked according to the course of this world, according to the prince of the power of the air, of the spirit that is now working in the sons of disobedience.

"Among them we too all formerly lived in the lusts of our flesh, indulging the desires of the flesh and of the mind, and were by nature children of wrath, even as the rest" (Ephesians 2:1–3 NASB).

Three points are worthy of special attention in the light of our subject. First, we were spiritually dead before we received Christ and God brought us to life in the new birth. We had a different nature then — the nature of the children of wrath, the spirit that works in the children of disobedience.

Second, when we were in that condition, we followed the world, Satan and the old nature in our conduct. Notice that conduct was "according to" or in keeping with the behavior patterns of Satan and the world. Isaiah 14:12–14 reveals the self–centered and self–serving character of this conduct.

Third, as shown by the passages from Ephesians and Isaiah, we seek fulfillment of the desires of the flesh through self–effort. In the Isaiah verses, the devil is quoted as saying "I will . . . I will . . . I will . . . " until he had reached the ultimate: "I will make myself like the Most High." In Ephesians, Paul says those who have not been saved walk, live and indulge themselves to fulfill the desires of the flesh.

Perhaps this is why Paul labels the fulfilling of these desires as "the works of the flesh" (Galatians 5:19 KJV). It is done by human effort and wit, by works. This is in sharp contrast to the manner in which the desires of the heart are fulfilled for those who have been born again as children of God.

How Are the Desires Fulfilled?

The first step in having the desires of the heart fulfilled is to determine the desires. Proverbs 3:5–6 holds the key to making that determination. You must: "Trust in the Lord with all your heart And do not lean on your own understanding. In all your ways acknowledge Him, And He will make your paths straight" (NASB). 1 Corinthians 2:10–14 says that the Holy Spirit reveals to the Christian's regenerated spirit "the things freely given to us by God" (NASB).

To determine the desires of your heart, you must let the Holy Spirit reveal them to you. Set aside an hour when you know you can be alone, sit down in a quiet place with a pen and paper and simply ask the Holy Spirit to show you the real desires of your heart. As things come to mind, write them down immediately so you won't forget them.

When desires stop coming to mind, review the list and thank God for revealing your desires. Tell the Lord that you are going to assume these are the true desires of your heart, as given you by the Holy Spirit, until He shows you in some unquestionable way that they are not.

The second step is found in Psalm 37:5 and 7 immediately following God's promise to fulfill the desires of your heart: "Commit your way to the Lord, Trust also in Him, and He will do it . . . Rest in the Lord and wait patiently for him; Do not fret because of him who prospers in his way, Because of the man who carries out wicked schemes" (NASB).

First: commit your way to the Lord. Present each desire to Him to be fulfilled. If it is done, it will have to be done by

Him. Self–effort is the program for fulfilling the desires of the flesh, not the desires of the heart. However — and this is important — you must also present yourself to Him; God must have you available to work with. Finally, you must present yourself toward the fulfillment of your desires.

The faith walk is not a passive experience; it is a walk. For most desires to be fulfilled, there are certain obvious things that must come about. For example, if you desire to become a musician, you must get an instrument, take lessons, practice and so forth. Your part is to present yourself to appropriate all of the necessary elements, depending upon God to give the provisions and to give you the required wisdom, talent, opportunities, health and perseverance.

Second: trust in Him and He will do it. Many Christians stumble at this point. They commit a desire to the Lord, but in presenting themselves toward the fulfillment of the desire, they forget to rely on the Lord for all that is required to fulfill it. We are

Any gift from God is a spiritual gift, whether tangible or intangible, visible or invisible, large or small.

especially vulnerable to this failing when nothing seems to be happening or we don't seem to be moving toward the fulfillment we expect. We tend to have preconceived ideas about how and when desires will be fulfilled. If progress doesn't measure up to our expectations, we tend to take over and begin trying to make things happen on our own.

Having committed our desires to Him, we must trust Him to fulfill them. We must rely totally on His power, wisdom and provision. Putting self-effort back into the picture shows a lack of faith. God will not honor a doubting mind: "But he must ask in faith without any doubting, for the one who doubts is like the surf of the sea, driven and tossed by the wind. For that man ought not to expect that he will receive anything from the Lord" (James 1:6–7 NASB).

Before God will fulfill our desires, we must believe that He will do it. As Jesus put it in Mark 11:23–24:

" 'Truly I say to you, whoever says to this mountain, 'Be taken up and cast into the sea', and does not doubt in his heart, but believes that what he says is going to happen, it will be granted him. Therefore I say to you, all things for which you pray and ask, believe that you have received them, and they will be granted you' " (NASB).

We lose the chance to have our desires fulfilled if we rely on anything other than belief. This is well worth noting because of the strong Pharisaical tendency that permeates modern Christian teaching and preaching. That tendency binds many to the idea that they must do something to merit having the desires of their hearts. This is in no way to belittle disobedience, but if you wait until you "get your house in order" before presenting your desires to the Lord, you will probably never have them fulfilled.

The preeminence of belief over works, sinlessness or any other factor in God's scheme of action is emphasized throughout the Bible. God used and blessed heroes of the faith such as Abraham, Jacob, Moses, Gideon and Samson despite obvious weaknesses and lapses in conduct. How does it so easily escape us that the "Hall of Fame" message in Hebrews 11 states clearly that it was "by faith" that the great deeds of these ancient figures were done?

When the children of Israel were at Kadeshbarnea, after Moses had led them out of Egypt, God told them they could go into the Promised Land and possess it (Numbers 33:50–53). He did not deny them that privilege later because of their sinfulness. In Hebrews 3:19 we find a blunt explanation of why He did not let them in: "They were not able to enter because of unbelief" (NASB).

God did not grant Solomon's desires on the basis of his perfection. 1 Kings 3:1–3 reveals that he had formed a marriage alliance with the Egyptian Pharaoh's daughter and that he was still sacrificing in the "high places." Neither of these things was in God's will. Yet God granted Solomon's desires because he was willing to believe in God and trust Him to do it. The idea that we must "clean up our act" before God can do anything for or through us is a relic of that former nature which operated on the assumption that acceptance is granted only on the basis of performance and merit. The believer is saved by faith, not works; the believer is under grace, not law.

"But God insists on righteousness," you may be saying. Yes, but He provides the righteousness (2 Corinthians 5:21). It comes only from Him, by faith (Romans 4:5). We couldn't work it up even if we tried; God doesn't want us wasting our time and His in that futile effort. He wants us to present ourselves to Him as living sacrifices (Romans 12:1). When the sacrifice is in His hands, He does the rest in His own time. Paul uses all passive verbs when speaking of what happens after the sacrifice is presented (Romans 12:2). This is what God does for the sacrifice, not what the sacrifice does for God or for itself. The work of sanctification is His through Christ (I Corinthians 1:30).

> *We are to "draw near with confidence to the throne of grace."*

When Christians try to work up their own righteousness, they revert to the pattern of the Jews whom Paul spoke of in Romans 10:3: "Not knowing about God's righteousness and seeking to establish their own, they did not subject themselves to the righteousness of God."

In so doing, they miss the liberating benefits inherent in verse 4: "Christ is the end of the law for righteousness to everyone who believes" (NASB).

God gives righteousness in response to commitment and faith, not our works or our flawless performance records. We have it from the lips of the Master in John 7:18: " 'He who speaks from himself seeks his own glory; but He who is seeking the glory of the One who sent Him, He is true, and there is no unrighteousness in Him' " (NASB).

As Christians, we have Christ, the one of whom that was spoken, as our life (Colossians 3:4). If He is our life, then He is also our desire. "Your name, even Your memory, is the desire of our souls. At night my soul longs for You, Indeed, my spirit within me seeks You diligently" (Isaiah 26:8b–9a NASB).

Because of our oneness with Him, we are sure that the motives of our hearts are to seek the glory of God, and not the fulfillment of self-centered desires. God has taken care of the righteousness requirement for us. By giving us Christ's life, He has seen to it that there is "no unrighteousness" in us. That frees us to be open to whatever he chooses to do in our lives to fulfill the desires of our hearts!

It also meets the "condition" attached to God's promise to

fulfill the desires of our hearts. Psalm 37:4 says, "Delight yourself in the Lord; and He will give you the desires of your heart" (NASB). Deceived by the leaven of the Pharisees, many believers have allowed Satan to turn this condition into a cruel taskmaster. What must we do to delight ourselves in the Lord? How could we ever know whether we have done enough to delight the Lord? That condition, like any other that pertains to our relationship with God, has been met through Christ. He has delighted the Lord (Matthew 3:17 " 'This is My beloved Son, in whom I am well-pleased' " NASB). When we believed in Him, He became God's delight for us!

Finally, in Colossians 2:9–10, we find that in Christ "all the fullness of Deity dwells in bodily form, and in Him you have been made complete" (NASB).

So Christ is truly all in all: He is the desire of our hearts; He is the delight in the Lord that meets the condition for the fulfillment of the desires of our hearts.

Once you have committed your desires to the Lord, and are trusting in Him to fulfill them as you present yourself for their fulfillment, you may rest assured that God will carry out His promise of Psalm 37:5: "He will do it." He will do whatever it takes to fulfill your desires. What remains for you to do? That is your final word of instruction: "Rest in the Lord and wait patiently for Him" (Verse 7 NASB).

What a magnificent formula for having your desires fulfilled: you commit them to the Lord, trust Him with them, He fulfills them for you, and while He is doing the work, you simply rest and wait!

Summary

In conclusion, to have the desires of your heart fulfilled requires only that you:

1. Pray, allowing the Holy Spirit to reveal your true desires.
2. Commit your desires to the Lord, trusting Him to fulfill them.
3. Rest and wait for Him to fulfill them, understanding that rest does not mean waiting passively but presenting yourself toward the fulfillment of your desires in dependence on God's power, wisdom and resources, instead of your own.

I cannot overemphasize the necessity of simply trusting God. The story of Jabez found in 1 Chronicles 4:10 reveals the importance of this truth:

"Now Jabez called on the God of Israel, saying, 'Oh that You would bless me indeed and enlarge my border, and that Your hand might be with me, and that You would keep me from harm that it may not pain me!' And God granted him what he requested" (NASB).

Nowhere else in the Bible is Jabez mentioned, except in the verse immediately preceding. Verse 9 says that he was "more honorable" than his brothers. What do you suppose made him more honorable in the eyes of God? In light of the fact that it is belief that pleases God (Hebrews 11:6), might it not be that Jabez simply dared to ask God for what he desired and to believe that he would receive it?

If you, too, were to show such faith, don't you believe God would be just as quick in saying to you, "Request granted"?

Dare to claim His promise to fulfill the desires of your heart. In doing so, you will actually fulfill a desire of God's heart. For that is precisely what He yearns to do for all His children.

Notes

Notes

Notes